HEALTHY BOUNDARIES

HOW TO SET STRONG BOUNDARIES, SAY NO
WITHOUT GUILT, AND MAINTAIN GOOD
RELATIONSHIPS WITH YOUR PARENTS,
FAMILY, AND FRIENDS

CHASE HILL

CONTENTS

YOUR FREE SAY NO CHECKLIST

DON'T LET THE PEOPLE PLEASING TRAP YOU AGAIN...

I'd like to give you a gift as a way of saying thanks for your purchase!

This checklist includes:

- 8 steps to start saying no.
- 12 must-dos to stop feeling guilty.

- 9 healthy ways to say no.

The last thing we want is for your mood to be ruined because you weren't prepared.

To receive your Say No Checklist, visit the link:

www.chaschillbooks.com

If you have any difficulty downloading the checklist, contact me at chase@chaschillbooks.com, and I'll send you a copy as soon as possible.

INTRODUCTION

What's the first thing that comes to mind when you hear the words 'healthy boundaries'?

Are you drawn to images of testing relationships and suffocating parents? Or is it a picture of frustration because your boss asks too much of you or your friends are demanding?

They are two words in the English language that so many of us strive for, but are often met by a brick wall. Every attempt to climb the brick wall results in a setback, pain, embarrassment, frustration, and fear of trying again. You know that if you could just get high enough to see over the top of that wall, life would improve. However, the idea of making another attempt prevents you from dusting yourself off and taking the next step.

Before you start to kick yourself when you're already down, think again. Struggling to establish boundaries doesn't mean that you missed this vital life lesson, or that you lack the intelligence to learn.

There are so many factors that contribute to setting boundaries, and none of them are your fault. We live in a bit of a dog-eat-dog world, and instead of supporting one another to the top, we are trampled on by the over-ambitious. Manipulation blurs the boundaries we are trying to set; not to mention the state of communication skills today.

Once upon a time we could have a face-to-face conversation, read body language, and understand tone of voice. Today, we often have to translate the meaning behind a combination of emojis. All of this culminates to make it harder to firmly establish our boundaries, and will be discussed in more detail later on.

The fact is, you do have to dust yourself off and learn how to set healthy boundaries. There's no way around this. Without them, you have no control over your own life. You end up doing things that make you unhappy, or even depressed. You can't say no for fear of hurting someone, and it's just easier to say yes despite hurting yourself. But deep down, you also know that it is neither fair nor right for you to continue to live a life that you can't enjoy to the maximum.

But it is far from doom and gloom! You don't have to continue living in a cycle that prevents you from reaching the top of your wall. From this moment forward, you can make the decision to learn new skills, master techniques, and show others that your boundaries do exist.

Everything you need in order to do this is here in this book.

Several years ago, I was in the same position as many of you are now. I was working in the corporate world and had a lovely girlfriend, my parents were caring, and my friends were supportive. Or so it all seemed.

My life felt like a pane of glass. From a short distance, everything was as it should have been. But there was a tiny crack – my lack of boundaries. The problem was that this crack expanded, and it wasn't long before my entire life was broken.

I had reached a point where I couldn't keep feeling like I was the least important person in the room. I suffered too much when my girlfriend constantly put her own needs ahead of mine. I was doing the hard work, and my colleagues were getting the glory and the promotions. My friends and family looked at me in pity, and instead of helping, tried to tell me what to do and how to live my life. I was literally facing the very bottom, and all too often, the bottom of a bottle.

Depression led to health problems, exhaustion and weight gain, and the confidence I needed to set the necessary boundaries was draining from me.

One night I was scrolling through social media, and I saw a quote that just hit me. "A lack of boundaries invites a lack of respect."

I was truly feeling that lack of respect, but the quote also reminded me that while I wasn't asking for it, I wasn't preventing it either. So, I typed in 'healthy boundary quotes,' and the next one didn't just hit me: it woke me up. "Stop asking why they keep doing it, and start asking why you keep allowing it." I may not have realized it at the time, but this was going to be my turning point.

I started researching the power of the word no. I looked into how people pleasing was something we misperceived as being nice, but really, it was the core reason for unhealthy boundaries. The combination of these actions, through no fault of our own, causes us to lead an unfulfilling life. But this realization was only the first step.

I confess it took me about a year to transform my life. Psychology became my hobby and my passion. I tried out strategies, and read up on numerous theories. I read, listened and observed. Sometimes, I failed, but when I did, I could still see the progress I was making. I made it to the top of my wall, and it was awesome! A new me is just too much of a cliché, and it was not even the case – I was the real me.

My confidence grew so much that I started helping others. This was more rewarding than any corporate environment, so I decided to change my career. My goal became to help others, not by telling them what to do, but by providing them with insight into the techniques I successfully used to turn my life around. The only difference is that you don't need to take a year to achieve the same.

My book, *Stop People Pleasing*, briefly touched on the topic of healthy boundaries, and it sparked a lot of questions from readers. For this reason, we are going to take an in-depth look at boundaries. Not just the different types, but also boundaries within different relationships.

Some of you will read this book so that you can become more confident at telling others what is acceptable and what isn't, to free up your own time, or to stop taking part in things you don't want to. Others might be looking for more respect, peace and love.

The journey may be hard, and it will require a close look at yourself and why you do the things that you do. The changes that we make aren't just to establish your boundaries: we are going to make sure that you can maintain them, even when those you love insist on pushing them.

At the same time, we are going to learn how to let go of the guilt that arises when setting boundaries, and how to free ourselves from the fear of losing people in the process of creating these boundaries.

I want you to enjoy this journey, understand more about yourself, and celebrate each win. Let's begin with the fundamentals of healthy boundaries.

CHAPTER 1: BEFORE WE START: WHAT YOU SHOULD KNOW ABOUT HEALTHY BOUNDARIES

B oundaries are the limits that we set for ourselves in a relationship. Rigid boundaries can create distance. Porous boundaries are weak, and often get crossed or violated. A healthy boundary is one where you can feel comfortable expressing your thoughts, feelings, and the word "no" so that you can appreciate closer connections.

It is always good to start by taking a step back and considering how you see boundaries. If you look at the traditional sense of boundaries, you might see them as limits, or a line you don't cross. And this is correct.

Some people are very good at staying clear of other people's boundaries, and others know the exact point that they can reach before they have gone too far. Sadly, there are others who have no idea of people's boundaries, and the worst situations to find yourself in are the relationships where people don't care about your boundaries.

Meanwhile, we have others who feel the need to constantly

push their own boundaries to succeed or to become a better person. Boundaries may also look like brick walls that we rely on for protection.

Before we go any further, ask yourself what your boundaries look like to you, and not what you think they should look like. If you're like I was at first, looking around trying to find your boundaries and realizing you don't have any, that's okay too.

This first chapter is about gaining an understanding of what healthy boundaries actually look like. So, regardless of what yours look like, from this point, we are going to give our attitude towards boundaries a clean slate.

We can classify boundaries as six key types: physical, emotional, time, sexual, intellectual and material (Earnshaw, 2019). Let's look at each one in more detail.

Your Physical Boundaries

Everything we need physically will have boundaries – from the food you need to the amount of sleep you require. These boundaries are defined by your personal space, as well as how much physical contact you're comfortable with. Physical abuse is an extreme violation of one's physical boundaries, but there is no question about when the line is crossed.

A physical boundary I had to work on personally was with food. I am what you could call a fussy eater, and although I'm happy to try new foods, I hate it when people try to force it on me. When someone started repeating, "Go on try it, you don't know if you like it unless you try it," I would always find myself caving in, and that would make me angry at myself.

Physical boundaries should include knowing when you need to rest or take some time to yourself. Peer pressure to go out in the evening or to attend family occasions on your day off are both examples of crossing boundaries. We are all entitled to take the time we need to recharge our batteries.

Personal space is high on the list of difficulties with physical boundaries. When Auntie plants a sloppy kiss on your cheek, she means well, but it makes you feel uncomfortable, and the line has been crossed.

This is a particularly important issue in the workplace. There are people who are naturally touchier – we call them huggers. Their physical contact is the same as another person's handshake. They might even find the thought of someone not liking a hug to be preposterous. Then there are the people who enjoy seeing you struggle when your personal space is invaded.

Your home is also important when you're thinking about your physical boundaries. Someone insisting on coming in is leaping over that limit.

Surprise visits can either be very welcoming or tread close to the line, especially if you already had plans but your visitor seems to feel they are more important.

Examples of physical boundaries:

- Being able to take rest when you need to

- People respecting your dietary needs

• Having the right amount of physical contact for the type of relationship

• Having personal space in your home

Your Emotional Boundaries

Our emotional boundaries need to be set with respect to how we are feeling, and this works both ways.

There will be emotional things that you will feel happy about sharing, and others that you would prefer to keep to yourself. Friends and family should be aware of exactly what you're comfortable talking about.

Parents and other family members have a wonderful habit of doing and saying things that embarrass us, whether that's getting out the baby photos, or reminding you that the clock is ticking and you should be settling down. Usually, this is fine but if it upsets you, there should be a boundary here.

Friends, too, need to know what you're comfortable listening to, but what's more, they need to appreciate your emotional state and whether you can handle taking on their emotional strains.

I am a firm believer in equal rights, equal earnings and equal housework, but we can't forget equal emotional rights.

This is another area we will be looking into further, but regardless of your gender, it is your right to be able to set emotional boundaries and to have them respected.

One of the things that hurt me so much with the

relationship I had in my 20s was that I was laughed at for trying to explain that I was nervous or sad. It was as if, as a man, I shouldn't have these feelings.

When someone expresses their feelings, there shouldn't be any judgment, nor the need for justification. Emotions shouldn't be questioned or corrected.

If you're feeling angry, you should be allowed to express this, and not have someone say you are just tired or hungry.

Examples of emotional boundaries:

- Speaking openly about your views and opinions

- Not being told how you feel

- Sharing only what is appropriate

- Not having to justify your emotions

Your Time Boundaries

Once upon a time – and it really wasn't that long ago – we didn't all have cell phones to text and let someone know we were going to be late.

Don't get me wrong, I love modern technology, but time was more respected in the past. We made the effort to be on time. It might be picking your kids up, meeting your family or friends, or turning up at work, but time boundaries mean sticking to the agreed time.

It is rude and disrespectful to make someone wait. Every now and then, there could be a genuine reason, but if you feel that someone is constantly late or cancels on you regularly, they aren't respecting your time boundaries.

One action that you might not consider to be a violation of your time boundary is when you tell someone that you're busy, but then they continue to try to contact you. Again, as with being late, they might have honestly forgotten that you had plans.

If you feel like this is happening on purpose, however, then the other person is using manipulative techniques to play on your intentions, possibly trying to make you feel guilty for not spending time with them.

Another small gripe I have with modern technology is the lack of respect for time boundaries at work. The pandemic has certainly not helped.

Our regular working hours are very much blurred, and with email, social media, group chats and video conferences, so many people are struggling with the pressure of work, with little time to disconnect.

Employers shouldn't ask for more than the contracted time, and employees need to ensure that they're completing tasks within the deadlines.

Examples of time boundaries:

- Arriving on time

- Respecting other people's time limitations

- Accepting when people can't make an event

- Keeping planned arrangements

Your Sexual Boundaries

This is another boundary that I feel very strongly about, and it's a challenging one. Young people may struggle to have the necessary conversations to practice safe sex, both physically and emotionally.

Even adults can find themselves in situations they would rather stop, but lack the courage, or feel that there comes a point where they can't say no. It may surprise you to think that sexual boundaries change with life events such as pregnancy and menopause.

Thanks to some amazing support networks and better education, rape is becoming less of a taboo subject. However, society still seems to view sexual assault as a crime only against women.

Shocking statistics show that one in 33 men in America has experienced attempted or completed rape (RAINN). And that is only those who are brave enough to come forward. The same studies highlight mental problems such as PTSD, increased risk of drug use, and problems with personal and professional relationships.

Violating someone's sexual boundaries includes lying about contraception or sexually transmitted diseases. Complaining when someone doesn't want sex or about a person's preferences, likes or desires is also wrong.

Withholding sex as a form of punishment may not seem like you're crossing this imaginary line, but it is still a form of manipulation.

Whether you're walking down the road, or you're in a club,

pub or at work, you must feel like you are in a safe environment, free from unwanted advances. If you choose to wear a short skirt, it doesn't mean you want men to leer. If you're a man without a shirt on, you shouldn't be subjected to sexual comments.

Examples of sexual boundaries:

- Asking for consent and respecting when the answer is no

- Talking about contraception

- Being open about sexual health issues

- Discussing likes and dislikes

Your Intellectual Boundaries

Have you ever met a person who is incapable of seeing things from your point of view? Or someone who fakes interest in your opinions, but always wants to be right and have the last word? Let's not mistake an education for intelligence. Anyone can read a textbook or watch a documentary and believe they are all-knowing about a subject.

Intelligence is a combination of intelligence quotient (IQ) and emotional intelligence quotient (EQ). A well-rounded intelligent person has the ability to share their learning, views and opinions, and then respectfully listen to others. They are willing to spark a conversation and even to debate, but they will never cross the line that makes you feel stupid. I was constantly interrupted by my ex.

It was infuriating, but I was never able to set the right boundary. My ideas were met with a look that told me I was just an idiot whose opinions didn't count, whether it was what take-out to get or the color of the wall. I'm no Einstein, but I'm not stupid, and although I have come a long way, crossing intellectual boundaries can be devastating for someone's confidence.

Intelligence boundaries include knowing when it is the right time to talk about certain topics. Religion and politics are banned from my family dinner table – just because there are too many differing opinions, and it's not the right time. If your partner does something to upset you, there's no need to shame them in public when you could talk about it privately at home.

You also need to be aware that setting intelligence boundaries means that you don't tolerate people's opinions on matters that are hurtful. Laughing with the crowd at a sexist or racist joke will probably go against your core values. Nobody should have to pretend to be someone they aren't just to fit in.

Examples of intellectual boundaries:

- Accepting that everyone is entitled to their own opinions
- Agreeing to disagree
- Knowing the right time to talk about things
- Not belittling people for their beliefs

Your Material Boundaries

This is a tricky one. We are taught from a young age that sharing is good – let others play with your toys, or give your sibling a sweet. You let your friend borrow your car, knowing they will leave their trash in it. The fact is, as adults, we have worked hard for our material possessions, and rather than seeing it as selfish and not sharing, it is more likely that we are protecting our investments.

Living with others brings up a lot of material boundary issues. If you're working from home, it's logical to set up a boundary regarding your computer. If someone breaks it, you could lose your income.

I feel a little weird complaining when someone uses my glass or my cup. It is enough to make others smile at what seems like a quirk. But these objects have meaning to me, and if they were damaged, I wouldn't be able to replace them.

Examples of material boundaries:

• Not taking things without permission

• Returning things in the proper condition

• Accepting a "no" when people can't or don't want to lend you things

• Respecting return dates

———

The aim of our first chapter is to awaken ourselves to the extent of boundaries. Take some time, and give yourself credit for those boundaries that you feel you have established. This might be the smallest thing like not letting your partner swear, or stopping your mom from packing up leftovers.

It's also about identifying the boundaries that you need to create. Now that you're aware of the different boundaries, we can start to assess which boundaries you need, and which ones you need to work on.

How to Practice Boundary Awareness

In your journal or on a piece of paper, draw seven boxes. Label each one as one of the boundary types, and the 7th as 'Other'.

You might want to take a week so that you have both working days and the weekend for a complete look at your relationships. Observe your week, and make a list of all the boundaries you can see that exist in your life.

Don't worry about looking at the boundaries you're missing: we'll start to work on this in the following chapter. Look at your relationships, and observe the boundaries you have in place.

CHAPTER 2: TESTING YOURSELF: DO YOU REALLY NEED TO SET BOUNDARIES?

Everyone needs boundaries. They are like our own little rule books. When you picture your boundaries as rules, it becomes easier to understand their importance. You can't play a game of Monopoly or football without rules.

Boundaries, like rules, help us to understand the thoughts, feelings and wishes of others, which in turn, allows us to maintain healthy relationships.

When our boundaries are clear, we are able to enjoy our personal and professional relationships. It is motivating to imagine saying no to someone and have them respect your answer.

Boundaries mean you will be heard and appreciated, and that your needs will be met. Healthy boundaries are mutual, meaning the other person will also feel safe within the relationship.

Needless to say, there are some situations when people aren't going to be aware of your boundaries and they might be violated. When a stranger stands too close to you, this is not on purpose. When you meet new people, they aren't going to be aware of where your limits are. Crossing them, again, is not intentional, and later on, we will look at how to establish boundaries in new relationships without causing offense. Then, we have those relationships that are well established but lack boundaries – often these the most challenging, as you may need to assert yourself more.

As I mentioned in the first chapter, we always need to go back to the foundations before we can start rebuilding. Now that you have discovered the extent of boundaries, it's time to figure out if you need to set them. It sounds like an obvious statement, but as a life coach, I have seen so many people who knew that they were in a toxic relationship, but they had never been able to put a finger on where it was going wrong. They were unaware of the need for boundaries.

What Do Unhealthy Boundaries Look Like?

After looking at what healthy boundaries are, you can imagine what unhealthy boundaries look like, some being more subtle than others.

- Giving inappropriate gifts

- Excessive texting, calling or emailing

- Ghosting

- Asking personal questions

- Repeating confidential information/gossiping

- Eavesdropping

- Imposing religious or political beliefs

- Demanding things of people instead of asking

- Interrupting

- Outbursts of uncalled-for anger

- Intimidating body language/communication

- Telling lies

- Saying yes to please everyone

- Feeling guilty about saying no

- Falling in love too quickly

- Not standing up for yourself or being afraid to disagree

- Trusting too easily

- Putting more into a relationship than the other person

- Expecting or needing others to care for you

- Pushing down your feelings or blocking them

- Letting others control your life

Let's take a closer look at some ways boundaries can be violated before further self-assessment.

What Do Boundary Violations Look Like?

- Physical contact that is not permitted

- Sex without consent

- Physical/emotional abuse

- Manipulation

- Taking belongings without permission

- Sharing confidential information without permission

- Posting photos on social media without permission

- Bullying, mockery, insults

Intimidating body language can be interpreted in more than one way, and it will depend on the other person's intentions.

Unfortunately, there are people in the world who are just terrible at communication and are unwilling to learn. These people are unaware that they're using too much eye contact and you feel uncomfortable. This is still a violation of your boundary, but you need to look away in the hope that they mirror your example.

The person who purposely shakes your hand for too long or kisses your cheek too close to your lips needs to be stopped. It is not possible to list all violations of boundaries because it is something that is very personal.

You might feel like all lies are completely unacceptable, but your neighbor might feel that a little white lie is okay to protect someone.

This is the gray area we all need to explore until the black and white become clear.

What Happens When You Don't Set Boundaries?

Some of the consequences of not having boundaries are as clear as day, and you will find yourself nodding as you read on. Personally, I found that life just hurt. There is a weight that you can't shift, an exhaustion you feel all the time. It can be hard to get out of bed knowing that you are about to face another day of feeling used or hurt. Some people are amazing at putting on a mask so that from the outside, they seem fine.

Because we feel that the needs of others are more important than our own, it's easy for others to take advantage. This lack of balance causes the 'dominant' partner to feed on the weaker.

Here too, there is a spectrum of signs. Subtle signs could be controlling what people wear. It doesn't have to be phrases like, "You can't wear that." When you notice your partner making frequent comments about what they prefer you to wear or what they don't like, they're crossing a boundary.

Verbal abuse, physical abuse or sexual abuse is a clear line that cannot be crossed whether you are male or female. If a woman hits you or if a man insults you, it is abuse. It is unacceptable, undeserved, and a sign of a toxic relationship.

After an extended time of not having clear boundaries, you will start to see a negative impact on your health. This may include lack of sleep, eating the wrong foods, burnout, drug and/or alcohol abuse, depression, anxiety, and self-harm.

The scary thing I worry about is that we all have our

breaking point. The moment when you know you can't cope with it anymore. We will learn how to set the necessary boundaries, and although your self-esteem is probably at rock bottom right now, you can do it. That being said, if you feel that you have reached your breaking point, please get professional help.

Setting boundaries isn't easy, and you need to start with the right mind frame and a can-do attitude. There is no shame in asking for support to get yourself in the right place to start working on these strategies.

How Do You Know if You Have Boundary Issues?

It's not always obvious, especially when it comes to those boundaries that are still a little gray or you haven't clarified your limits around just yet. Below, you will find 20 questions that you can use as a form of self-assessment. You can give each question a score from 1 to 5, 1 being never, and 5 being always.

There is no golden answer here. Mostly nevers might mean that there is just a small area of your life that you would like to improve. If everything comes back as always, it's time to wipe the slate clean and create fresh, strong boundaries. If you end up with a lot of sometimes, it probably means your boundaries are there, but you need to reinforce them.

Remember that nobody is going to correct your answers or judge you, or even see them, so be completely honest with yourself.

1. Do you regularly feel stressed, anxious or overwhelmed?

2. Do you feel like you aren't in control of your life or that

others tend to control it for you – kids, partner, parents, etc.?

3. Do you feel like there is always something that needs to be done or that you are always behind on things?

4. Do you feel like your loved ones take advantage of you, your time, your generosity, etc.?

5. Do you go out of your way to prevent others from being hurt?

6. Are the needs of your loved ones more important than your own?

7. Do you feel that people won't want to be with you unless you meet their needs?

8. Do you attend to the needs of your family and friends before your own?

9. Do you resent your loved ones when they ask too much of you?

10. Do you feel like you need to justify your needs, whether that's to others or to yourself?

11. Do you feel obliged to say yes because you're the only person who can help?

12. Does it upset you or hurt you when you think you have let others down?

13. Do you worry that people will leave you if you say no?

14. Is it easier for you to just say yes to avoid confrontation?

15. Do you doubt your feelings, assume you don't have the right to these feelings, or feel that your feelings aren't as important as those of others?

16. Does it make you anxious when you think people don't like you?

17. Does it make you anxious when people don't approve of you?

18. Do you believe other people's criticism, without considering the circumstances?

19. Are others able to control how you feel by playing with your emotions?

20. Do you find yourself making excuses for others or covering for them?

I love to use these questions for general boundaries. Further on in the book, we will look at specific types of relationships, and this will enable us to look more closely at whether you need to work on your boundaries.

If you still feel like you're unclear on your boundaries, don't worry. In the next chapter, we're going to dive deeper into defining your boundaries to provide complete clarity before creating strategies to set them.

CHAPTER 3: 7 DEEP QUESTIONS TO HELP YOU DISCOVER YOURSELF AND CREATE BOUNDARIES

"Life wasn't meant to be easy. The difficult things we go through are the things that make us stronger."

— KOMAL KANT

We can find 100 quotes about the necessity of doing the hard things in life. The lesson is normally that life is better once you have mastered a skill, and the difficult task then becomes easy. Mastering your healthy boundaries starts with some difficult questions, but the sooner you start, the better off you'll be. This is because, as time passes, the people around you become accustomed to treating you in a particular way – the way you don't like.

If you feel like you're facing an impossible challenge and have no idea where to start, it's time to take a deeper look at yourself and what the real you looks like.

This is not supposed to be a session where you look at all your negative qualities so that you feel worse about yourself. If you find yourself starting to get frustrated with yourself or upset, take a step away, or you will find that your discoveries won't be constructive.

Rather than overwhelming you, we are going to look at different types of boundaries, but in each situation, you will be able to see three clear stages.

We will follow the 3 C system – Create, Communicate and Control. It is wise to make sure you have the 3 Cs in your plan before enforcing boundaries, but we will look at each extensively.

Learning to Define Your Boundary Limits

These questions are designed to help you clearly identify the thin line between what matters to you and what you are comfortable accepting.

It is the first stage of our 3 Cs in creating boundaries. You are the only person who can create healthy boundaries, but starting with the answers to the following questions will help you find your limits. Only when you know what is valid to you will you be able to explain these validations to others.

Take a piece of paper and a pen so that you can make notes. Don't feel like your answers need to make sense straight away. Take two shots at deep questions. The first time I write down what immediately comes to mind. I call this the unfiltered stage, or the raw answers. Sometimes, it doesn't seem that my thoughts make any sense. Then I take a little more time to really delve into the question.

It's a good idea to try to find a peaceful moment to ask these deep questions. Don't feel like you need to do this all in one sitting. It's better to take a day or two rather than to rush through. Revisit the questions when you're in different places or when you're with different people. Make a note on your phone, and then add it to your piece of paper later. The more ideas, thoughts and opinions, the better – as long as they're honest!

1. What are the positives and negatives of your relationships?

This in itself is quite an extensive question because there are numerous relationships to consider, each with its own boundaries. Your list of relationships could include your partner, children, friends, parents, other family members, your colleagues, your boss, etc.

Try to keep your list quite specific because your relationship with your best friend might not be the same as with other friends. You may prioritize their needs differently – just as you might be comfortable with a kiss from your mom but not so much from cousins or aunts.

2. Do you do things out of love or fear?

This is a great question. Look back at the last 10 or 15 things you did for other people. It doesn't matter who these people are or the size of the task. Decide your reason for saying yes. Was it because you wanted to, because you love that person and doing it made you happy? Or did you do it because you feared the repercussions of saying no?

3. What makes your blood boil?

The answer to this question will help you to define your hard boundaries. These are the boundaries that will not be crossed no matter what.

Most typically, these actions go against your core values. They might be racist comments or jokes, unfaithfulness, inequality, or breaking the law. It could also be things like people telling you how to raise your children, or arguing with you about topics that you feel passionate about.

4. If you had unlimited time and money, what would you do?

This is not a question to spark a daydream. The reality is that you will have to get up for work tomorrow, and winning a lottery is unlikely.

The idea behind this question is to consider the daily things that make you happy, whether that be reading more books, going to the cinema, or going out for dinner more often. It is these things that you frequently don't get to do because you are unable to say no to helping others.

5. What's on your bucket list?

I've seen people pull a strange face when I ask them this question. They seem to think it's depressing thinking of things that they want to do before they die. Realistically, it's just the list of things you want to do and achieve in life.

Your bucket list could include travel, a fitness goal like running a marathon, extreme sports, learning how to cook, overcoming a fear, or seeing the Northern Lights – the list is endless, and it should be motivating. Having a list of your own goals will help you to see the importance of putting your own needs and dreams before those of others.

6. What did you love doing as a child?

Children have hobbies. For so many of us, adulthood can mean sacrificing our hobbies for responsibilities. Those long bike rides become evening routines. Movie nights are replaced with working overtime. The list goes on.

The moment when I realized I had no hobbies was quite shocking for me. How do we get to this point? To fix this, go back to the things that you used to love as a child. Which hobbies would you like to start again, or do you have others in mind that you fancy trying?

7. Are you a human being or a human doing?

This is deep, but the answer is one or the other. There is a wonderful Buddhist proverb, "When is more enough?" Our lives are filled with things we need because we think they will make us happy.

You have to say yes to your boss because you need the money. You allow your friends to decide what the plans are because it is easier than rocking the boat. This is a human doing (Saviuc, 2020)!

You are defined by what you do. By the end of this book, you will be able to enjoy life as a human being, be who you really are, and start to live life to the fullest.

Let's look at how one person answered these questions and how he used the answers to start developing his boundaries.

Example Answers to Help You Put the 7 Questions Into Practice

Luke has been struggling with understanding his boundaries for a while. He has attempted to set some and enforce them, but people either assumed he was joking, or they just brushed off his requests. Here are the notes I took after reviewing Luke's answers:

Question #1 - What are the positives and negatives of Luke's relationships?

Luke is single. He knows that he doesn't want to start another relationship until he is stronger. He has a daughter with his ex, and sees her once a week. Her mom has a habit of changing the day to suit her, and he is scared that by saying no, he won't be able to see his little one. His parents are generally understanding, but every now and then, he feels like they still treat him like a child, which prevents him from wanting to do more with them. His best friend is his rock, and is always telling him to stand up for himself. He has distanced himself from other friends, and regrets this slightly.

Question #2 - Does Luke do things out of love or fear?

His biggest fear is not seeing his child. The other things he has done for others recently have been in order to have an easy life: neither love nor fear.

Question #3 - What makes Luke's blood boil?

It is his work environment that makes his blood boil at the moment. There is a toxic atmosphere where certain employees can break the rules, and the others just have to pick up the pieces. It's not enjoyable, and he knows that he wants to do something but is unsure of what steps to take.

Question #4 - If Luke had unlimited time and money, what would he do?

Luke would love to spend more time exploring nearby cities and cultural areas, perhaps take some day trips to meet new people. In general, he would like life to slow down a little bit, perhaps be able to sit in a coffee shop and watch the world go by.

Question #5 & 6 - What is on Luke's bucket list? What did he love doing as a child?

Luke wants to swim with dolphins, walk part of the Great Wall of China, and go on a short cruise. As a child, he loved playing football in the street with his friends, and he loved his pet fish.

Question #7 - Is Luke a human being or human doing?

Luke is definitely a human doing. He felt that each day of his life was a process to be completed. He had fallen into a routine, and couldn't see a way of breaking it.

From this incredibly deep look at his life, Luke could see that his feelings were not valid. Despite having tried to talk to his ex and his parents, their behavior continued. He knew that his best friend would be there to support him, and he was interested in reconnecting with other friends if could be sure the boundaries would be in place and respected.

Work would be a challenge. Answering the question reminded him of how much he loved his job. He didn't want to look for another job because that would feel like running from the problem. He would still need boundaries in a new work environment, so although he was nervous, he was determined to find a solution for work. He decided to use the items on his new hobbies and bucket list as rewards for achieving various steps throughout his journey.

Turning These Questions Into Practice for You

Finally, with all of your newfound information about yourself, draw a line straight down the middle of a piece of paper.

This line is your boundary. It is your absolute no, and from this moment, you can no longer make exceptions. To the right of this line, write a list of everything that is crossing your new boundary. Don't hesitate. If you don't feel that people respect your emotions or needs, it goes on the list. If your boss doesn't respect your weekends, it is written down.

To the left, you can now place ideas in relation to the line. If your mom insists on you taking home Tupperware lunches, think about this for a second, or even ask her. Is she doing it because she thinks you can't take care of yourself, or is it because she simply has leftover food not to be wasted, and thinks it will save you time?

Suddenly, what you saw as overstepping a boundary might just be a case of a mom being a mom.

There will be some things you don't mind doing. If your friend needs you for an emergency, you can put this closer to your line. The idea is to create a visual image of what is acceptable and what is not.

For many of us, understanding our boundaries is hard because it is not something that we can physically see. This paper provides a visual tool. You can always edit it, add new boundaries as new situations come up in life, or adjust one, as long as it is a decision you want and not something you feel like you have to abide by.

We're still at the point where the work we're doing toward our healthy boundaries is just for you. I think this is an important thing to keep in mind because if you start to worry that others will see your notes or your boundary line, you won't be completely honest.

Even if it is subconsciously, you will start to create new boundaries that will make others happy instead of yourself. You may even start to feel guilty at the idea of someone reading your thoughts and feelings; you might feel like you are being selfish.

Negative emotions such as guilt and the fear of saying no are huge influencers on our ability to create healthy boundaries. So much so that the next chapter is dedicated to finding your inner strength to overcome these negative emotions and to actually look forward to creating boundaries.

CHAPTER 4: POWER WITHIN: HOW TO STOP FEELING GUILTY, OVERCOME FEAR, AND FIND ENERGY

This is one of my favorite stages in the journey to enforcing healthy boundaries. It requires a change of mindset, meaning that you must expand your ideas on common issues that often prevent us from putting ourselves first.

Often, we know what our boundaries look like, especially after the previous chapters, but there is still a stage in the middle that is essential if we are to succeed with these boundaries – the strength and power to say no without feeling guilty or selfish.

The Real Reasons That Some People Don't Have Boundaries

#1 Reason: People call me selfish when I try to set boundaries.

Solution - Changing your mindset will help. The reason we need boundaries is so that we can take care of our health. You wouldn't be called selfish if you went on a diet or saw a doctor when you needed antibiotics. Selfish is when you constantly put yourself ahead of others, not when you put your wellbeing first.

#2 Reason: It is just easier to say yes.

Solution - In the short term, it is easier to say yes. But, in the long run, you will continue to suffer mentally and physically, and probably worse than you are now. At first, it will take more energy to assert yourself, which is why it is essential to take care of yourself. However, once you have passed the initial stress, you will find it gets easier to say no.

#3 Reason: Even though I know the relationship is bad, I am scared of ending it.

Solution - Ending a relationship is always going to cause fear. You might fear being alone or fear the idea of being independent. The fact is, you deserve better, and the fear is often about the act of ending the relationship rather than what comes next. Take some time to plan how you will achieve your goals and the rewards.

#4 Reason: I don't set boundaries because I worry that my family will love me less.

Solution - Establishing your boundaries isn't about creating distance. It's about communicating your wishes and needs in the right way so that your family don't take offense, but understand the importance of your boundaries.

When boundaries are set in the right way, you have the chance to experience greater love.

#5 Reason: People will see me as boring.

Solution - The word 'boundaries' does have a mature sound to it, but that doesn't mean you're boring or that you're uptight. Without boundaries, you may end up without the strength or energy to enjoy any time with your friends and family. Saying no to the things you don't want to do will provide you with the energy to enjoy the activities that you want to do even more.

#6 Reason: I can't set boundaries because people need me.

Codependency will often prevent people from creating their boundaries, and unfortunately, this leads to others taking advantage of them.

We will look closely at codependency for different relationships, but it's important to understand the difference between supporting others and doing everything for them.

I feel that a large part of this problem starts in childhood and follows us into our adult lives.

Even though it was almost three decades ago, I can still remember the pressure in high school to make friends, to be popular, and to be liked. It is part of human nature and the way we are wired, so there's nothing wrong with this.

It goes back much further than this – it is a survival tactic. It's hard to deny that babies are just adorable and cute. They need adults to see them this way so that they are taken care of.

Research on parenting styles also impacts our view of

boundaries from a young age. In the 1960s, Diana Baumrind noticed that there were three major parenting styles: the authoritative, the authoritarian, and the permissive (Parenting for Brain, 2021).

Authoritarian parents have extremely strict rules and a somewhat black and white approach, which can result in children growing up with low self-esteem. Permissive parents are often over-indulging, and there are few or no rules.

A child's behavior can be egocentric, leading to problems in relationships. It is the authoritative parents who are warm and supportive, yet have clear rules and high expectations. This parenting style creates higher self-esteem and improved social skills.

Social media has taken the need to be liked to an extreme level, with people defining themselves by the number of likes they have. When people say that social media has become a drug for them, they aren't exaggerating.

Dopamine is a chemical that is released when we do something that feels good, and it will motivate us to do it again. It is produced when we have sex, when we exercise, or when we do any other enjoyable activity.

Cognitive neuroscientists have shown that receiving likes on social media causes an influx in dopamine.

Racheal S. Heslin, transformational author and speaker, likens our need for approval to the small part of us that still fears what we did as a child – the need for our parents' love and approval. It is only when you are able to provide yourself with the approval that you need that you can start to forget the recognition you crave from others.

The need to be liked and loved becomes a problem when you have to do things that you don't want to do for fear that someone will like or love you less.

This causes us to do things we wouldn't normally do. If you think about it, it's probably the worst thing we can do when starting any kind of new relationship.

I remember on one of my first dates, my then-girlfriend insisted that I tried fish in a restaurant. I hate fish, but I wanted to impress her, so I tried it. From that very moment, the boundary had been crossed, and it would be hard to undo the behavior.

To be liked, it can often feel as if we need to be this chilled out person who goes with the flow. You don't want to come across as the party pooper, so you say yes to everything. The price you pay for not being boring is people taking advantage of you.

It's also true that some of you have been able to say no, but the reactions from people have left you feeling worse than you would have if you'd just said yes.

I've been called selfish, mean, and even heartless after trying to say no. My ex had fits of rage followed by tears. I would have to back down because I felt responsible. She would smile, and only then would I realize that it was all an act.

It is often similar in the workplace. Have you ever tried to say no to your boss or colleague and then experienced micro-actions that feel as if you're being punished?

By definition, they are so small – being left out of a group email or having ideas dismissed in a meeting – that you might think you're being paranoid.

Being liked and loved is no different for an empath. The difference is seen in the degree in which they experience other people's emotions in a relationship.

Highly sensitive people will experience love in a different way. It might be deeper, rawer and more beautiful, yet more painful at the same time.

On the contrary, narcissists seek out those who they can get the most from. It is still a need to be loved and liked, but it can almost come across as though it is their right, often not caring that their partner (often an empath) also has needs.

To overcome these challenges, we have to break down this stage and first work on our confidence and skills to express our needs.

We are also going to learn that setting boundaries isn't selfish at all; in fact, on the contrary, you are helping those in your life to have more meaningful long-lasting relationships.

Taking Care of Yourself to Boost Your Energy and Inner Strength

We all know that it takes an awful lot of energy to deal with certain people. Unfortunately, dealing with them results in burnout, anxiety, stress, and a whole handful of other potential health problems. It is likely that you aren't sleeping properly, and you wake up extremely tired. It's easier to grab an energy drink for that boost of energy you need rather than looking for long-term solutions. There's no judgment here: I have been there.

However, all of these health problems cause us to look at ourselves in a different light. The extra pounds we might be carrying all of a sudden make us think we're fat and ugly. The bags under our eyes make us look drained. Every negative knocks our confidence, and we start to tell ourselves that we don't deserve to be happy. For this reason, it's time to start taking better care of yourself.

Don't panic! No strict diets or hour-long sessions at the gym. Here are some ideas that you can easily add to your day so that you start increasing your energy and boosting your confidence:

• Drink more water. Start the day with hot water and a slice of lemon. It is a great cleanser. For every coffee you drink, have a glass of water first, and another glass with each meal.

• Try to add more fruit and vegetables to your day. I confess, I love a chocolate cookie, but I made a rule where I could only have one if I had a piece of fruit with it.

• Increase your mood-boosting foods. Things like Omega 3, dark chocolate, bananas, berries and nuts can help you to feel more positive about life.

• Exercise is essential. I promise I'm not a fitness freak, and I'm not pumping weights at the gym every night. Exercise makes me happy, even if it's a short walk each day or 20 jumping jacks and a few yoga stretches to start the day. More oxygen is delivered to your organs, including your brain. You will have more energy and better concentration.

- Start meditating. Meditation is no longer the same hippy concept from the 70s. Scientific studies are continuously showing the health benefits of meditation, including managing stress, reducing negative emotions, and increasing patience.

If you find meditation hard, you can find excellent guided meditations online. I absolutely love this guided meditation for confidence. Marisa Peer includes some wonderful phrases that relate to our boundaries, such as "You matter," and "You are significant."

Scan the QR code above to open the meditation.

If you can't open it, please use this short link:

http://bit.ly/meditation-01

- I recently added the Wim Hof Method to my daily routine, and the results were outstanding. Today, we aren't so in touch with our basic survival needs. We have resources that help us when it comes to food and clothing. Not being in tune with the need to survive reduces our ability to connect with our inner self, where so much of our power lays dormant.

Here is another guided video that will teach you the Wim Hof Method. If you feel that this method is going to help, it's worth downloading the Wim Hof Mobile App. The free version lets you watch videos, practice exercises, and monitor your progress.

Scan the QR code above to open the Guided Wim Hof Method Breathing video.

If you can't open it, please use this short link:

http://bit.ly/wimhofg

• Create to-do lists. I have a daily to-do list that I write with my first coffee of the day. It helps me to organize my thoughts and prioritize. Crossing off completed tasks shows the progress I have made, and it helps to motivate me throughout the day.

• Take 5 minutes for yourself every day. I know you're busy and there are plenty of other things that you can do with those 5 minutes, but it is doubtful that those things are more important than your health.

Step away from the technology, read a couple of pages of your book, or stand outside and breathe in the fresh air. Just 5 minutes all to yourself is a small step to allowing your needs to matter.

• Create a bedtime routine. In order to get a better night's sleep, be strict with your evening routine. Needless to say, you should avoid caffeine, but try to keep your phone away from your bed too.

Overcoming Negative Emotions to Establish Boundaries

The two main negative emotions we feel when setting boundaries are guilt and fear.

Guilt arises because we have put our own wishes before others, and the second we do this, we begin to feel as if we are selfish. It is possible to feel guilty because the other person needs you, or just because you have come across as being mean and not caring.

Fear can be brought on by short-term consequences, like someone is going to get angry with you or insult you, or long-term consequences, like fearing losing the person from your life.

Let's tackle the two separately.

Tackling Guilt Head-on

Never have I seen a worse case of the guilt trip than the Rolo advert from the 90s. You know, the round caramels covered in chocolate wrapped in a tube. The voice would say, "Do you love someone enough to give them your last Rolo?"

And this resonates through our entire lives as we live with this idea that we have to walk on burning coals to prove our love for someone. Anything less, and we feel guilty.

It is just as bad when we are able to say no without guilt, but then the other person says something or acts in a way that causes us to start feeling guilty. Neither situation warrants this guilt.

Why should you feel guilty for doing exactly the same thing the other person's doing when they don't guilty about it? What makes their needs more important than yours? Is it just because they are better at dramatizing their needs?

Setting boundaries is nothing to feel guilty about because it is teaching others that there has to be a balance in the relationship, some give and take. It is what successful relationships thrive on. You're entitled to your thoughts, opinions, beliefs and emotions, just like the next person. You are no less worthy.

You also can't feel guilty for putting self-care ahead of the wishes of others. An important part of having boundaries is to recognize that we all have our limits, both physically and emotionally. You need to dedicate time to yourself so that you're in a better position to help others when they need it.

This is a very common problem for parents. Parents could spend 24 hours a day taking care of their children, making sure they're healthy, safe and happy. The thought of taking some time to do an activity they want to do is impossible because of the guilt.

Logically though, we all know that a 10-minute shower, a glass of wine with friends, or sneaking in an episode of your favorite series without the kids screaming at you would be enough to recharge your batteries. When you're able to see that self-care makes you a better person for those around you, it is easier to leave the guilt behind.

You will also find that freeing yourself from guilt is something that requires practice. As you begin to start setting your boundaries, if you start feeling guilty, follow these steps:

1. Take a step back, and stop talking. Take a deep breath, and give yourself a second to compose your thoughts.

2. Remind yourself that setting boundaries is a good thing. Find an affirmation that empowers you, a short phrase to help you remember that there is no need to feel guilty. Try sentences like, "I have done nothing wrong," "My boundaries are a good thing," or "My boundaries are important."

3. Don't apologize or feel you have to justify your words.

The more you talk, the more ammunition you give them to try to change your mind.

4. Keep in mind the activity you would rather be doing instead of what the other person is asking of you: it will help you to stay focused.

5. Smile. Smiling helps you to express your thoughts confidently, and without coming across as being mean.

6. Don't punish yourself if you still feel guilty. Time is going to help, but the initial goal is to have other people respect your boundaries. The more success you have, the less guilt you will feel.

7. Don't let setbacks put you off trying again. Sometimes we win, sometimes we lose, and sometimes the actions of others are so strong that it might not be possible to avoid guilt. This is on them, not on you, and it doesn't mean that you aren't able to set boundaries without feeling guilty.

As with so many of the techniques we master throughout this book, it is going to take strength and perseverance to overcome guilt. However, you will experience such an amazing rush with even the smallest progress that you will be motivated to keep going.

Getting to the Bottom of Your Fears

When breaking down the process of setting boundaries, it's important to discover which stage makes you afraid. So far, we haven't done anything that should cause real fear because we're still in the planning and preparation phase. You probably haven't put anything into practice. It's very rare to feel fear when creating your boundaries.

So now it's down to two other sources – expressing your boundary or the consequences of doing so. Even when you're expressing your boundary, the fear begins because you're already thinking about the reaction you might get. To take this one step further, we need to identify the type of fear (Levin, 2021).

Are you scared that the other person is going to get angry? Could it be because they might get upset? You might fear hearing the word 'no' or them rejecting you in some other way. And what if they were to simply just walk away?

This is the best thing about fear! We are afraid of something that doesn't exist, and this is how we need to rewire our brains to think. The moment that fear starts to fill your body, you have to tell yourself that the consequence of your boundary isn't set in stone.

The only sure thing is you expressing the boundary, and this is what you can control. By placing all of your focus on explaining your boundary, there will be no room for fearing what is yet to happen, if it even will.

Let's look at some methods for overcoming certain types of fear:

Fear of aggression - If you are in the extremely difficult position of trying to express your boundaries to an aggressive person, you might freeze in fear because of their possible reaction. It is essential that you deal with this type of person in a place where you feel safe. Ensure that others are around you, but they don't necessarily have to be people you know. Even being in a public place will reduce the likelihood of a violent outburst, and there will be help if you need it.

Fear of abandonment - Some of your loved ones won't like the idea of you creating boundaries you intend to keep. They might have lost their control over you, or they might not like the fact they are no longer the focus of your life. In some cases, they will threaten to leave, and in the majority of these cases, it is just a threat. They are hoping to create this fear of abandonment so that you revert to being your more submissive self.

Even though you can see that your relationship is toxic, it doesn't mean it is easy to end. You may start to worry about the possibility of being alone forever, or that in reality, you need this person. The truth is that you don't need this toxicity in your life. You are stronger than you realize, and with time, you will see this. Removing people who manipulate you will provide you with the space and energy to focus on who you want to become, and make way for better relationships.

Fear of shame and embarrassment - Worrying about being shown up in front of others is a frequent reason for delaying boundary setting. If you're out with friends and you say no to your partner, the moment they start to ridicule you is mortifying. All eyes are on you and how you react, which is something that people with our personality are generally uncomfortable with.

As you work through the stages of this book, you will start to see your confidence grow, and you will feel more empowered in these situations.

Remember, all eyes might be on you, but people are actually highly attuned to shaming, and as a society, we are becoming less tolerant. The audience will feel embarrassed for the other person's behavior.

Fear of stress - We already lead incredibly stressful lives. According to the American Institute of Stress, 75% of Americans experience moderate to high levels of stress. Stress infiltrates every area of our life. Avoiding it is a way of protecting our physical and mental health.

The stress we fear when developing our boundaries is a necessary evil. We need to work through this stress because the result will be less stress in the long run.

Taking care of yourself is critical, which is why we closely examined ways to make yourself stronger in Chapter 4.

Simple Steps to Overcoming Your Fears

The following steps are very simple. However, that's not to say that you will wake up one morning and your fears will have just disappeared. It might take just a couple of days, or maybe a few weeks, but practice is the key.

• Get to the bottom of your fear. Understand the type of fear and where it is coming from.

• Listen to your fear. You can't just block it. Take time to address it. Don't feel like you have to take action straight away – a few minutes for reflection will help to calm your subconscious.

• Focus on your goals. Your goal is a firm boundary, but beyond that, it is a more fulfilling life. This positive visualization can gradually replace the fear and provide you with motivation.

• Make a decision to learn from your fear. Fear causes pain, but this pain offers us a chance to grow. Learning to let go of the pain helps to overcome present and future fears.

• Understand that, on occasions, you will fail. Not everything in life is about winning or succeeding. Failing is not the same as being a failure. It is a minor bump in the long road. When fear rises up, concentrate on deep breaths, and never give up. The rewards will far outweigh your little setbacks.

The majority of our fears are based on experiences from our past. It might be that you have tried to tell a co-worker that you won't pick up their slack and they ignored you, and now you fear that any time you attempt to assert yourself, you are going to get the same reaction.

And here is the beauty: you will now have the skill and confidence to establish your boundaries, so the chance of people reacting inappropriately is greatly reduced.

Furthermore, as I have said before, you are only able to control your actions and emotions. In the case of others reacting the wrong way, you have to accept that this is their problem rather than your failure.

How Can Empaths Protect Their Energy and Create Boundaries?

Empaths or highly sensitive people (HSPs) aren't just highly sensitive to physical and emotional stimuli. It is believed that they have a more sensitive central nervous system, which enables them to literally take on the emotions of others, making boundary-setting especially difficult. Not only do they have their own emotions to handle, but they also take on the reactions of those with whom they wish to create boundaries.

An empath can already feel stress and fear; expressing their needs can lead to them absorbing the upset or anger of the other person. It is estimated that approximately 20% of the population is highly sensitive (Scott, 2020), so you aren't alone.

While it is easy to see the downside of being an empath, you have to remember that there are positives. You have the ability to appreciate things at a much deeper level, whether that's the emotions felt watching a movie or documentary, or the more profound connections you can make with friends and family.

At the same time, creating boundaries is also going to be much more difficult... but it's not impossible. Here are some things that empaths should take into consideration regarding healthy boundaries:

• Certain social situations may be more stressful, as you will be able to pick up on a huge range of emotions that others may not.

• A busy schedule can cause you to feel extremely overwhelmed, unlike others who are able to thrive on the stress. The thought of not being able to achieve everything generates stress.

• Since you are more aware of others' feelings, it is

incredibly hard to say no and feel the disappointment of your friends or family.

- Empaths will avoid conflict whenever possible.

- Empaths may struggle more to end a toxic relationship. You might feel that there is more to be done before walking away.

- Empaths are prone to rumination, continuing to think about a stressful situation, with thoughts turning more and more negative.

Many of the techniques we have looked at will help highly sensitive people, but there are specific things that you can incorporate in your life to make you feel more comfortable about creating boundaries.

1. Protect your energy

The first thing is to protect your energy. If you have taken the steps to start boosting your energy, it is important that you don't let others drain it away. If you know certain people who we call energy vampires, keep a distance from them. If you are in a social situation where you pick up negativity, politely move away.

2. Use visualization techniques

At this stage, you can use visualization techniques to create an image in your mind of the boundary issue you have. Take a look around the situation – what is happening, and how do you feel?

Think about the changes in your energy and the energy of others. Repeat this activity for a few days. Each time, you will start to notice more details. This self-awareness will help you to face challenging situations in the real world.

3. Consider your boundaries

We have already done this. Take the notes you have made previously, and now focus on the energy concerning these boundaries. Because you will be more sensitive to the energies surrounding a boundary, you might need to adjust them.

4. Say no to the big ones

There are probably lots of cases where you want to say no, but of course, it's going to be hard taking on all of those emotions. Reserve your energy for the no's that matter. Depending on the situation, you might use phrases like, "I see your point of view, but I don't agree," or a simple "no." There will be plenty more on how to say no later in this book when we look at specific relationships.

5. Have faith in your instincts

It is easy to not trust your gut feeling when so many thoughts and feelings are swirling around. Listen to advice, but always remember that you know yourself better than anyone else does.

6. Create a safe space in your home

I call this your charging dock. A space that is full of positivity and warmth. This happy space is where you can go to escape the stress of the day or the world. Take 5 minutes to meditate or practice mindfulness to balance your energy.

7. Self-love is even more essential

Absorbing other people's emotions is going to be extremely draining. Whatever it is that helps you to relax must be part of your daily routine. It could be cooking, listening to music, dancing, drawing, fresh air, or anything under the sun that means you are your own priority.

Please don't think that this is the end of the help for empaths. As we continue on our journey, I will make sure to include specific tips and strategies related to the topic we are discussing.

How to Deal With Codependency

Codependency is a complex learned behavior (Gaba, 2019) , often developed in our early years. We have watched a parent or family member who has displayed codependent traits, and more often than not, they were matched with a narcissistic partner.

It is the codependent who goes out of their way to satisfy the needs of the other partner. So much of the attention is on the needy person and the efforts to please them that other people in the family learn quickly that their needs will always be the lesser priority.

Many of the struggles we have discussed ring true for a codependent – they will fear loss and confrontation. They might not be aware of their own needs, or they may feel that their needs aren't as important.

Codependents can also feel quite isolated. People outside the relationship will tell you to stop being a doormat, but it is just not the case. A learned behavior takes time and practice to reverse.

If you have grown up in a verbally, emotionally or physically abusive family, you might need cognitive behavioral therapy (CBT) to help change the negative patterns that codependency has created. This is a great way of discovering the difference between your needs and problems, and the needs and problems of the other person.

Relationship dynamics may determine the way you face your boundary-setting, so in the next few chapters, we will look at how codependent people can successfully create boundaries for various relationships. For now, here are some general guidelines for setting boundaries in a codependent relationship:

• Be explicitly clear when communicating your boundaries

• Let others know how their codependent behavior makes you feel

• Be there to support codependent people, but don't do everything for them

• Wait for a request for help rather than offering

• Don't tolerate any form of toxic behavior

• Teach others the importance of self-care by being a great role model

• Make codependents take responsibility for themselves and their actions

This chapter has focused on the need for self-care and self-love. We have looked at the importance of understanding that it is not only okay to put your emotions and needs ahead of others in your life, but it is also your right to do so.

Gradually, you will start to feel more confident within yourself, and more determined about maintaining your boundaries. What is going to help even more is knowing exactly what to say so that your loved ones respect your words and don't get upset by them.

CHAPTER 5: POWERFUL BUT KIND WORDS FOR EXPRESSING YOUR BOUNDARIES TO PEOPLE

I f you have read any of my other books, you will probably remember that I am an advocate for teaching soft skills in school. I know there's so much that teachers already need to include in their curriculum, but how can we forget the importance of communication skills? We are still working on the assumption that we pick this up naturally; however, it is far from the case.

There are two factors to consider when understanding why we all need help with communication, neither of which are bad things. With increased globalization, the world is becoming smaller. It is far easier for us to travel, and people are more comfortable with living and working in other countries.

We are exposed to a wide range of cultures, which is fantastic when it comes to expanding our knowledge and understanding of the world. But each culture has its own mannerisms around communication. Some men would be shocked if another man from a European country gave him two kisses on the cheek. It would most definitely be a violation of a boundary. But the European man might find this shocked reaction offensive. There are hundreds of examples of cultural differences that have changed the way we communicate.

Technology is another. It is such a shame to see people in cafes and bars all on their mobiles instead of having a face-to-face conversations. I worry that we're heading towards a world where we forget how to express our feelings in person because it's easier to hide behind a text message.

This chapter is going to teach you how to master communication, the second of our 3 Cs, in a way that allows you to explain to people your boundaries using kind words, and not feeling the need to be aggressive.

We're going to look at the fine line between passive and aggressive, and look at the most effective ways to say no. Our aim will be to improve our communication skills in person. Nevertheless, throughout the book, we will also discuss situations where modern technology can help us to communicate our boundaries.

What Does Healthy Communication Look Like?

I like to break communication down into three sections. Naturally, our words are going to have a huge impact on how we communicate our boundaries and how the other person reacts. Next, we need to learn just how much our body language impacts our communication. Finally, we will understand the importance of listening, rather than hearing what we think is being said.

How to Successfully Communicate Boundaries

The whole book has tips and techniques for very specific situations, but here we will look at the guidelines to communicate your boundaries in a way that leads to the desired results.

Step 1 - Know exactly what you want to say. You need to remain specific and clear. Your statements shouldn't be long, or contain any type of hidden meaning; nor should the conversations start to wander off topic.

Step 2 - Use I statements. There are two core reasons for this. First, you need the conversation to be about your emotions and not the actions of the other person. Second, I statements prevent you from making assumptions about the other person's feelings.

Step 3 - Listen to what the other person has to say. Don't interrupt them, and don't assume you know how they're feeling or what they're thinking. Repeat what they have said so that they know you're listening.

Step 4 - Be aware of each other's triggers. When people start to swear, I get mad. This is my trigger, and I have to be careful not to react negatively when others swear. Being aware of triggers will help to prevent the conversation from taking a wrong turn.

Step 5 - Make your expectations clear. Half of the boundary is how you feel; the other half is the behavior you would like to see changed.

Step 6 - Apologize when necessary. Saying sorry isn't a sign of weakness. It is admitting a mistake has been made, and showing that you would like to put things right.

Step 7 - Accept that people are going to have different opinions and it isn't possible to agree on everything. You might need to take a break from the conversation and come back to it when you have both had a chance to think.

To put these steps into practice, you could try some of the following clear examples of communicating your boundaries:

● I don't like it when you won't let me finish what I'm saying. I need to feel like we're equals.

● I feel like you're obliging me to do things when you start a sentence with "You have to…" I think there are better ways you can ask for my help.

● I'm sorry that you feel this way, but I need to be able to express my feelings without you taking it personally.

● We're both entitled to our thoughts on this subject, but I don't think we're making progress. Perhaps we can talk about it again tomorrow.

How to Set Limits and Still Be a Loving Person

This is another case of what might seem like a fine line. The word "no" can sound very harsh, and perhaps too direct for some people. On the other hand, if your words are not firm enough, the other person might not respect your boundary.

First, let's look at some ways that you can express a

boundary in the wrong way, and some of the ways you can express it the right way.

Sarah has a boyfriend who is constantly interrupting her. It makes her mad, and she admits it's hard to control her temper. She will often use phrases like, "You're impossible when you're like this, and it's not worth talking to you." This comes across as an insult, and naturally, her boyfriend often throws an insult back.

Instead, Sarah could say, "I'm listening to what you're saying, but I feel disrespected when you don't listen to me." The emphasis is no longer on his behavior, but on her feelings.

James has a colleague who takes all the credit for joint projects. He has used sarcasm to try to keep the tone light, but still express his dislike. His colleague has taken the sarcasm as a joke, and continues to reap the rewards.

His kind words to set the boundary would be, "I really enjoy teaming up with you, but I don't feel that there's a balance. What can we do to fix this and work better together?" This is a great sentence because the colleague has heard the positive and the problem, and James has asked for feedback towards the solution.

Eli's friend wants her to commit to a plan every Saturday morning. She already has a 50-hour job, and her parents aren't in the best health. She is exhausted, and has told her friend that she can't. Her friend might complain and call Eli selfish, but this is very much out of character.

In this case, Eli should ask her friend if there's an

underlying problem. If this is typical behavior of the friend, Eli could say, "I'm not selfish. I love you, and I am happy to do X activity on Y day. But I'm not going to commit to Saturday mornings." The boundary has been set, the insult has been corrected, and an alternative has been provided that they can both be happy with.

Question: I'm not sure about how to set boundaries so that we both get what we want and need and still be happy.

Answer: Communicating your boundary isn't just about expressing your needs and then ending the conversation. In order for both parties to be happy and to feel that there is a healthy balance in the relationship, it's important that you listen to the other person's response and maintain positive communication until you find the middle ground.

How to Say No Without Being Rude

A fellow life coach once said, "If you want more time, freedom and energy, start saying no." In essence, it is that simple. Nevertheless, this tiny word can pack a lot of punch. Even the idea is enough to make some people feel nervous and stressed – even sick to the stomach.

For many of us, it is the word "no" that makes us feel as if we're being rude. It is hard to go from someone who constantly says yes to a person that comes out with a straight no. The good news is that not all boundary setting is going to require a firmer hand, and a lot of people will respect your answer without having to use the word "no." For example:

- Now isn't a good time.

- I have a full schedule today.

- I can't.

- Right now, that isn't possible.

- I'm available tomorrow.

- Today isn't going to work for me, but how about next week?

- I need time to think about it.

- I'll think about it.

- Sadly, I have plans.

- It sounds great, but maybe next time.

There will be times when people don't accept this answer, or they have a more dominating personality, and will require you to be firmer with your boundary-setting. Always remember that no is not a bad word when used in the right way. You can use any of the phrases above, but start it with a no. Also, don't forget things like "No, thank you," or "No, sorry."

Question: When I say no, people look at me as if I don't have the right to. Then they insist on me explaining myself or justifying my answer.

Answer: There will be times when people insist on pushing against your boundary. Stand firm. You are not obliged to defend your no or explain your words. Choose phrases like:

- I don't appreciate it when you insist on me explaining

myself.

- You should accept my answer and not badger me for more details.

- What I do with my free time is my business.

- I'm not obliged to explain myself to you.

- I'd prefer not to say.

- I have my reasons

For those who aren't used to seeing you stand up for yourself, you might need more than one attempt for the boundary to sink in. It doesn't mean you've failed or that you're destined to back down. If you do feel yourself wavering under the pressure, this is perfectly normal, but don't give in for an easier life.

One good way to prevent a yes from slipping out when everything in you wants to say no is to ask for more time or information.

Ask questions about what the other person is asking of you. Then tell them that you'll think about it. Once you walk away from the pressure of the situation, you can decide whether it's something you want to agree to.

Explanations are dangerous ground. I have a general rule where the fewer words said, the better. The longer we talk, the more we say, and the more we say, the more opportunities the other person has to change your mind.

Imagine a conversation where you start listing all of the things you need to do. The other person is going to start organizing your time. All of a sudden, you have to run errands after work, the kids can go with their grandparents, and the ironing will just have to wait.

If you had kept your response to a simple, "No, I can't," you would have maintained control of your own time. At the end of the day, it is exactly that – your time!

How to Handle People Getting Upset With Your Boundaries

Not everyone is going to get angry with your new boundaries. Some people might get upset because they assume that you don't want to spend time with them. It can be particularly difficult if they become so upset that they start to cry, and even more so if you're an empath.

In this case, it's important for you to remind people that the boundaries are not because you want to end a relationship or to create distance. Let them know that it's the opposite. Having healthy boundaries is the key to continuing a healthy relationship built on honesty and respect.

Be wary of those who turn on the waterworks to make you feel guilty. This is a manipulative technique they're using in the hope that you'll change your mind. Regardless of the authenticity of their upset, you still shouldn't allow people to disrespect or cross your boundary.

A Sound Check for Your Tone of Voice

It's worth bearing in mind that only 7% of communication is based on the words we use (Albert Merhabians' 7-38-55 Rule, 1971). That's not to say that there's no point in carefully selecting your phrases. Being confident in what you want to say will help you to come across as more confident in your decisions. A massive 38% of our communication is down to our tone of voice.

As we go through some different tones of voice, have a think of people you know, and see just how accurate the description is.

A deep tone of voice, whether the speaker is male or female, implies that the person is more mature. You might find that once the voice becomes too deep, there is an element of darkness, even depression. It weighs heavy on your ears. A very quiet tone of voice shows that someone is lacking in confidence, they are shy, or they are nervous about something.

When a person's voice is incredibly high-pitched, it is difficult to take them seriously. People who speak slowly show a lack of interest, whereas rapid talkers might be trying to hide something.

A tone of voice that is neither too high nor too low, too loud nor too quiet, with calm breathing, suggests confidence.

To practice your tone of voice, record yourself on your phone. It can be reading a few sentences from a book, or some of the boundary phrases we have looked at.

When you play back the recording, the first thing that comes to mind is, "Oh... that's what I sound like!" But everyone has this moment.

Now bring your attention back to the descriptions, and see which areas you need to tweak.

How Small Changes in Your Body Language Can Reinforce Your Boundaries

Our words are only going to be as effective as possible if we're able to match our body language to the same message. Mixed messages are when your words plant a firm boundary, but your body language is submissive. 55% of our communication comes from our body language.

There is a great amount of psychology behind body language, and I must admit I find it fascinating. One of the best things you can do before putting these ideas into practice is just to spend some time watching other people's body language. Often, people say what others want to hear, but body language can paint a more honest picture.

Another thing to practice is self-objectification. This is when we try to imagine what others think when they look at us. Empaths may have an advantage here.

Really, it is something we all do at some point. When you look in the mirror, you're checking to see how you look, but as you don't look at yourself all day, really, you're looking at what others are seeing. This is a good technique to check that your body language is relaying the same message as your words.

However, be careful not to get stuck in self-objectification mode. Studies show that self-objectification can take us out of the moment and make it harder to concentrate. When expressing your healthy boundaries, you definitely want to remain in the present.

Have a look at the following questions to see if you are mastering positive body language.

Do you know what *iHunch* is?

The "i" refers to smartphones, the hunch is a slouched position. When you look at someone on their phone, you'll notice that their head is down, they're leaning forward, and their shoulders are slumped. If you have the iHunch position, you're suggesting that you're disengaged, but it's also a very submissive position.

How long are you holding eye contact for?

Too little, and you are not showing confidence; too much, and the other person might feel like you're flirting with them. The difference is a matter of seconds. Thanks to much research, psychologists have come up with the ideal level of eye contact for a confident appearance.

Eye contact should be made before the conversation begins. The ideal amount of time is 4 to 5 seconds (Schulz, 2012). The perfect ratio is to maintain eye contact for 50% of the time when you're speaking, and 70% of the time when you're listening.

Are you knitting your eyebrows?

Knitted eyebrows doesn't mean that they're tightly joined. It means that they're lowered and centered, but in a natural way. A little too far, and you will be frowning. Knitted eyebrows are a sign of focus and determination.

Is your head in line with your neck?

Nobody likes to see a person with their nose up in the air as if they're superior, but keeping your head down is another submissive gesture. Your head should be in line with your neck. Be careful that you don't nod in agreement without realizing it.

What are you doing with your arms?

Arms that are crossed show a lack of confidence, while folded arms are likely to portray a lack of interest. Your hands will also play their role. Closed palms or hands behind your back are signs that you're hiding something. If your palms are open, it shows that you are too.

Are you aware of the relationship between breathing and body language?

There are more advantages to deep breathing than bringing about a sense of calm and control. Breathing from your diaphragm is seen as more relaxed, and again, confident. As you're probably aware, when you're nervous or anxious, your breath becomes shallow and rapid.

Some of our body language is innate: we are born with it, and we can't control it. Blushing, for example, is going to happen whether we like it or not. Micro expressions occur at a fraction of a second, and also can't be controlled.

Everything on our list can be learned, which is excellent news because everybody has the ability to learn new things.

The first step to learning how to control your body language is to be aware of it, so after some time watching other people, turn your attention to yourself.

Focus on the way you stand in a supermarket queue, how

you sit at your desk, and your position when you're in social situations.

Start by making small adjustments. You could change the habit of crossing your legs and arms so that you appear more open. Or you may feel that your shoulders need to be less slouched.

Make the changes now, before expressing your boundaries, so that your body language backs up your powerful but kind words.

Why Should I Listen When I Want Them to Hear Me?

We have two ears and only one mouth for a good reason (Epictetus AD55-135)! The 60-40 rule suggests we should listen for 60% of our communication and speak for 40%. This might sound bizarre when we're working so hard on what we want to say, but listening is still an essential part of establishing boundaries that will last.

Imagine a conversation where you tell someone that you don't like it when they insult your taste in music and try and get you to listen to their favorite songs.

You have expressed your boundary correctly, and are revisiting the conversation in your mind while the other person is speaking. They might be trying to explain the reason why they think you would like their music.

Some people also have the habit of assuming what the other person is thinking, and therefore don't actively listen. Either way, not listening can cause the other person to feel hurt and disrespected – the exact thing we don't want for ourselves.

Listening to the other person's thoughts and feelings doesn't imply that you have to go back on your boundaries. It provides you with an opportunity to strengthen your relationship by addressing their concerns, and essentially, finding a middle ground.

You might tell your friend that you will listen to some of their music but you'd like them not to force it on you when you're not in the mood. Then reinforce the fact that everybody is entitled to their own tastes.

If you're the type of person who feels selfish because you're setting boundaries, effective listening will help you to overcome this: you are not making it all about your needs, but understanding the two sides.

Just remember that even listening should have its limits. If a person starts to shout, swear or become aggressive, it's time to let them know that you aren't going to listen to them while they're speaking in this way, and that you can have the conversation later on when they've calmed down.

What Not to Do When Setting Boundaries

- Never rush to set a boundary. You will find that your emotions are not under control, and you might not be fully prepared for the response.

- Don't lie. It sounds obvious, but we might tell lies in order to protect other people's feelings. It won't help because your boundary won't be true to yourself, and it won't be very clear.

• Try not to be inflexible with your boundaries. You will have your list of absolute limits, but remember there might be times when the boundary was crossed for a good reason.

• Remember that people are not perfect. Rather than focusing on mistakes people make with regards to your boundaries, check to see if they're making an effort to learn and respect them.

• You cannot forget to reinforce your boundaries. As we aren't perfect, it's likely that people will either intentionally or unintentionally cross your boundary. You will need to be both patient and determined in order to reinforce your boundaries.

———

How to Practice Communicating Your Boundaries

Before jumping into practicing communicating your boundaries, take some time to practice successful communication. Apart from watching other people's body language and listening out for different tones of voice, start taking some notes on your communication skills. Answer these questions:

• Do you think you're an active listener? Can you remember everything that people say in a conversation?

• Are you able to spot other people's triggers? Watch for tension in the body as a reaction to things you say.

• Do you interrupt?

- Are there any parts of your body that fidget or distract the listener when you get uncomfortable?

- Can you stop a conversation before it gets heated or out of control?

All of these are essential skills for communication, and for successful boundaries, effective communication is a must.

There is a huge amount of information in this chapter, and I hope you're motivated to start putting it into practice. Don't overwhelm yourself with too many changes at once. After some time of observation and self-reflection, make a list of things that you'd like to improve, and begin by making small changes. The small wins will encourage you to keep going.

We have looked at improving your lifestyle so that you feel more energized, and we've got to the bottom of our inner-selves, and are now fully aware of the boundaries we wish to introduce. With the tools to express your boundaries in a kind but firm way, you are now ready to bring everything together and start setting boundaries with your family.

CHAPTER 6: HOW TO DISCUSS YOUR BOUNDARIES WITH FAMILY

People around the world have their own definitions of family that often go beyond the traditional blood relatives. Your family might include parents and siblings, a partner and/or children. We have aunts and uncles, cousins, nieces and nephews. Some of our best friends can be more like family… and then there are the in-laws!

For this chapter, we are going to take parents, partners and friends out of the equation. This is because the dynamics of these relationships are quite complex, and we will focus on them in individual chapters.

The core boundaries we're going to look at are with siblings, in-laws, more distant relatives, and our children.

Siblings Who Overstep the Limit

Generally speaking, it is your sibling who knows you the best. At the very least, this was the case for the majority of your childhood. The massive amount of time you spent together provided them with the chance to know exactly what you like, how to tell what mood you're in, and of course, what annoys you.

Empaths, like twins, are likely to have an even stronger bond with their siblings. So why is it hard to create boundaries with the people who know you inside out?

As you're growing up together, the role model for boundaries is typically the parent. Children follow the words of Mom and Dad, and little attention is aimed at the siblings developing their own boundaries. As you get older, parents might start to say, "Figure it out yourselves," meaning that whatever problem you have, you need to deal with it together. This is the first stage at which you and your sibling establish boundaries.

The teenage years hit, along with rushing hormones and new sets of problems. Certain things that were acceptable no longer are – in particular, the concept of personal space and privacy. Younger siblings who have always just walked into a room are not used to now being shouted at and told to get lost.

The boundary is there, but it isn't expressed in the right way, and because it isn't expressed in the right way, problems will continue to not only occur, but increase in severity.

Things can quickly become toxic when a parent favors one child over another. In our minds, we tell ourselves that this isn't possible, but favoritism is very real.

A 2005 study showed that 74% of mothers favored one

child over the other, and 70% of fathers had a favorite child (Journal of Marriage and Family, 2016). The study was relatively small, with just 384 families and an age gap of fewer than 4 years. Nevertheless, the percentages are quite high.

Favoring a child is extremely dangerous, as the favorite learns that they can manipulate the parent, while the sibling is left feeling second best and less significant.

Whether or not your parent has a favorite child, you probably feel as if you weren't treated as an equal when you were younger, and your sibling has the ability to cross all boundaries. There's little point in playing the blame game, as it's unproductive. It's time to get to the core of the issue and change the behavior.

Before dealing with a toxic sibling, it is necessary for you to have your emotions under control. They're probably more than capable of knowing what to say in order to upset you or make you angry. You can't allow them to have that control over you anymore. Once they see that they don't get that rise anymore, you may find that they completely back off and move onto the next person.

Let your sibling know that you will no longer accept their behavior towards you. They shouldn't be allowed to think it's okay just because they're your sibling. It could be that they aren't aware of how much they're hurting you. This could lead to an open conversation about your relationship where you can both express your feelings.

Keep reminding yourself that you aren't the villain, even if they make you out to be. Explain how you respect their boundaries, and give clear examples like, "I don't call and gossip about you to the rest of the family," or "I respect that you need time for yourself."

Tell them that you love them, and you want them in your life, but not as the relationship is now. Paint a positive picture of the relationship with clear boundaries so that they can completely understand your reasons.

When siblings continue to break boundaries, you will need to have a more serious conversation. It might be that they weren't listening the first time around, or that they didn't feel that you were serious enough.

Change your vocabulary to make it more powerful, rather than angry or infuriated. Let them know that their actions will lead to consequences. Be careful that your consequence doesn't sound like a threat, as this can lead to confrontation.

Try to avoid phrases like, "If you don't do this, I will do that." You should try to phrase it more along the lines of, "If you keep crossing these boundaries, I don't feel like we're going to have the close relationship I want to have with you."

Finally, give your siblings a chance to improve their actions, and trust that they will make an effort. You might want to choose a time frame for this so that it doesn't go on for a long time.

After, say, a month or two, you might need to create some distance between you and your sibling. That's not to say that you should cut off all contact: the longer this goes on, the harder it will be to make things right. Some space will give you the time to feel stronger and give them a chance to think about what life would be like without their siblings.

Phrases to practice:

● I know you need my car, but you can't borrow it today. Next time, ask in advance.

● You know I'd love to, but today's not going to work for me. Rain check?

● I don't like it when you play Mom and Dad against me. It hurts.

● I would appreciate it if you didn't talk to the family about my private life.

● I can see that you're angry. I'll come back at a better time, and we can talk.

The Wonderful World of In-Laws

You might be one of the lucky ones who get on well with their in-laws, or you might not. Regardless, boundaries still need to be made. This relationship is often a complex one because of the subtle competition for attention.

As the most complex relationship is normally between a girlfriend and her mother-in-law, we will use this as an example, but this isn't to say that the same boundaries won't apply to other in-law relationships.

When a girlfriend comes along, the son's attention moves away from the mom, who had been the most important female in his life, to the girlfriend. Mothers often feel saddened that their son doesn't need them as much, and it can lead to jealousy.

Other moms might feel that the girlfriend is never going to be good enough for their son, or that they aren't going to be as capable of taking care of them. There are several issues with this, but the biggest is that girlfriends aren't supposed to be replacement moms, and it is not a girlfriend's job to take care of the son.

Caring is mutual and equal. Some moms have such tight control over their sons that their interference is a serious violation of boundaries.

The silly thing is that both parties have the same goal – the happiness of the loved one. And this is the key to enforcing the right boundaries with your in-laws.

While you have already concentrated on the boundaries you need for a happier, healthier life, you will need to start with the reasons for establishing these particular boundaries. Your in-laws might have a habit of making you feel bad about yourself, insulting you, disrespecting your opinions, or ignoring you. The tension could be so much that it's causing problems within your relationship with your partner.

If you're having trouble with your partner, you need to sort this out first. Any sign of a divide between you could be seen as a weak point and fuel the problems with your in-laws.

A good way to start looking at what boundaries to set is to create two lists: one for what you need, and another for what the family needs. It might be your wish to see your in-laws less, but that's not fair on your partner, and even less fair to the grandchildren. Once your two lists are complete, talk with your partner to create a set of boundaries that work for everyone.

You don't have to do everything together, so one solution would be for your partner to take the children for some visits, and you all go together for others.

When you and your partner are comfortable with the boundaries, it's time to have a conversation with the in-laws.

You can use the same short phrases we've seen before, but it's crucial that you use the word "we." If you use the word "I," your in-laws may feel that the boundaries are only coming from you, and they will feel as if you're controlling the relationship.

The stressful part comes when you have to maintain these boundaries. Watch out for your in-laws having conversations with your partner without you in order to persuade them to see things from a different point of view.

Also, be careful they don't use grandchild to tug on your heartstrings in order to cross boundaries. To prevent this, be prepared to adjust boundaries to accommodate their wishes, while making sure that you and your partner are still happy.

It's also worth considering your partner's relationship with your parents and whether there should be boundaries put in place to ensure your partner is happy. Don't assume you know the answer – communication from both sides leads to healthy boundaries for everyone.

Phrases to practice:

- We're so grateful for your advice, but we're going to go down a different route.

- We know the holidays mean a lot to you, but this time, we'll be spending them with my family.

- I'd feel more respected if you called before showing up.

- My job isn't to replace you. I'm his partner, and there's room for both of us.

- I don't like it when you spoil the children. Can you ask me first, please?

Having the Right Boundaries for Other Family Members

It's hard not to love your grandparents. I love how grandparents do all of the things that they would never have done with their own children, but feel fine doing it with the next generation. They're wise and have a different perspective on life.

Aunts and uncles are like parents, but again, they have a unique perspective and relationship with your parents. Then we have cousins, and if you're lucky enough, they're almost like extra brothers and sisters.

This isn't to say that setting boundaries is easy. It's true that you probably don't spend as much time with them as you do with your close family, and it's easier to break ties with those who constantly cross the limit.

But they're still family, and the one thing you notice as you get older (and go through pandemics and other life changes) is that you need your family. Let's look at some of the ways that family members can overstep boundaries:

• Talking down to you

• Disrespecting your values, ethics, or religious and political views

• Treating you like a child

• Nagging about you growing up, getting a job, or starting a family

• Trying to control your relationships

• Talking about you behind your back

• Showing up at your house unexpectedly

• Expecting you to go to family occasions

• Requesting too much from you

• Sharing your photos on social media

You can probably think of plenty more specific to your situation. While it's tempting just to accept that they're family and they only do it because they care, this isn't a healthy attitude, and it isn't going to help you on your journey to a better life. That would be like going to your favorite restaurant and having a glass of water – not really the point!

Choosing the right time to bring up your boundaries is critical to your success. At this point, family members may have pushed you to such an extent that you're a ticking time bomb. It might be that the next violation of your boundaries will cause you to explode.

The sad fact is that the attention will be on your explosive outburst rather than the behavior of the family member. And this is going to be worse if you're at a family gathering. Every excuse will be made for your outburst – the pressure of your job, your inappropriate relationship, or the fact that you aren't getting enough sleep.

Never do we hear, "I've overstepped a boundary, and this has caused your upset." Unwanted advice is a classic example. After all, they were "only trying to help," as we hear so many times.

So how do you find the best moment?

First of all, the frustration that leads to the moment when you can't handle more of your family takes time to build. Don't fall into the pattern of, "I will mention it next time." The next times keep building up until you can't take it anymore.

It's important not to let it get this far because it might not be the right moment to establish your boundary, and you need to know that the problem hasn't got to the point where you might lose control. Let's look at an example.

Joe has an uncle who keeps calling him a player because of the girlfriends he's had. In reality, Joe hasn't had an excessive number of girlfriends, but naturally, his issues with healthy boundaries are also affecting his relationships.

During his early 20s, this was kind of an acceptable joke that his uncle would bring up at every event. As the years went on, it was no longer the case of a young man sowing his oats, and the joke became quite hurtful when his uncle mentioned he couldn't keep a good woman.

Joe didn't laugh at the jokes anymore. His mom had picked up on Joe's sadness at being the butt of the family joke, and had also attempted to reign in her brother's seemingly harmless comments. Joe was able to control his emotions during family occasions, but each time, he dreaded these get-togethers more.

One day, while talking to his parents, he lost his cool, and this upset him further, so he decided that it was essential to enforce a boundary with his uncle.

At the next family occasion, Joe was prepared for the jokes. He had prepared what he wanted to say, and was prepared for the necessary conversation. Because he wasn't at his complete limit, he was still in control of his emotions and his ability to use the right words with the right body language.

As expected, the jokes were made. Joe was in the perfect position to take his uncle to one side at the right time, and explain how he was feeling. He said that although it was funny, it was causing him pain.

Boundary preparation was what enabled Joe to succeed, and it can do that for you too. His uncle apologized, and said he was unaware of the pain he was causing. Still, after years of habit, Joe did have to remind him of this boundary now and then, but each reminder became easier, to the point where just a look was enough for his uncle to stop.

If a family member gets mad because you've set a boundary, this is proof that the boundary needed to be set. Constantly remind yourself that you aren't a doormat for family members to walk on.

You shouldn't be the tool they need to achieve their goals, and you're certainly not the little child they still see you as. Look at the achievements in your own life to remind yourself that you're a responsible adult now. You have experiences and knowledge that you can contribute to your family.

It's a shame that there are times when family members don't respect our boundaries. It's not quite the same as a sibling or in-law.

If a family member insists on crossing the limits you've clearly set, it's time to create that space for your own wellbeing. It doesn't have to be forever. But if they aren't willing to understand the importance of your needs, happiness and life, you're better off removing them from the equation so that you can look after yourself.

Phrases to practice:

• It upsets me that I'm the butt of the family joke. If this continues, I don't feel like I can come to these occasions.

• This is not the time to discuss my love life.

- I know Granny isn't well, but she's not asking me to drop everything: you are.

- This conversation is inappropriate for a family dinner.

- I'm an adult, and capable of making my own decisions.

Getting Your Parenting Style Right for Healthy Boundaries With Children

Years ago, I was scrolling through Facebook, and came across a story of a mom who had reported her son to the police. Not knowing the woman on the street was his mother, he had come up behind her and mugged her. His intention was to use the money to feed his drug habit.

The mother had done plenty of research on codependency and setting boundaries, but nothing had worked. Her son had violated a boundary that was beyond acceptable, and the only solution was to report him. I found her story to be inspiring, and a sign of just how strong parents can be.

Hopefully, if you need to establish boundaries with your children, it won't be quite so extreme. Nevertheless, even pushing the limits can be exhausting. If you're living with your children, it's a problem that you can't escape from, and you may find that it impacts your health more.

We briefly talked about authoritarian, authoritative and permissive parenting styles. Now we're going to look further into the benefits of authoritative parenting and why this style is not only the middle ground, but also the most effective when setting your boundaries.

Don't think that it's too late. Adapting your parenting style can be done whether you have a two-year-old or a 20-year-old.

Before we get into the details, you need to know that what you've been doing up to now may not have been working, but that isn't to say you're a bad parent. Absolutely nobody in this world is a perfect parent: there are just too many factors. What does matter is that you want to improve.

A parent who is authoritative is one who actively listens to their child without dismissing thoughts, feelings and ideas. At the same time as respecting a child for who they are, an authoritative parent will set and maintain boundaries. They will understand the importance of give and take with a child, instead of setting rules that can never be broken.

Think back to when you were a child. It's natural to try to break the rules – it's what happens afterward that matters. The idea is to allow a child to explore rules and boundaries so that they can learn about limits and what happens when they're crossed.

If you think about an incident from your own life, you can agree that you learn more from trial and error than you do from what someone tells you. What's more, when someone tells you that you can't do something, you become more determined to do it. Children are no different.

It is this definition of an authoritative parent that allows for happy children who are comfortable in social situations and have better mental health.

To adopt this style of parenting, you need to start by listening to your child, no matter how old or young they are. When children express their feelings, be sure not to belittle them. It's true that their problems are probably not as important as finding the money to pay the utility bills, but to them, it's a big deal.

You need to have clear rules in your home, and it's common to have to remind children of the rules regularly. What's even more important is that any breaking of the rules, even minor, needs to have consequences. You have to remember that parents should punish the behavior and not the emotion.

A child expressing anger should be allowed to explain how they feel. But if they throw something in a rage or become physically violent, there has to be a consequence.

On the other hand, good behavior has to be rewarded. Don't mistake this for the permissive parent who overindulges.

Small rewards appropriate for their age motivate children to improve certain behaviors, and the parent is given the chance to help with support and positivity, rather than nagging and punishment (Morin, 2020).

Children are going to test boundaries. However, there are some cases where the problem gets out of hand. Family violence is on the rise, and it is not only child abuse and violence against women.

Studies in 2019 showed that between 7.2% and 22% of adults had experienced physical aggression from their adolescent children. For psychological aggression, it was between 65.8% and 93.5% (International Journal of Environmental and Public Health, 2019).

If, for any reason, you feel that you can't set boundaries with your children and they're physically or emotionally causing you pain, you should seek professional help.

When looking at establishing boundaries with different family members, begin by making sure you're clear of what these boundaries look like and if there's room for give and take, depending on your relationship and their expectations.

Prepare yourself so that you're in the right frame of mind and are feeling as confident as possible.

Finally, start with the people who you know will understand, and who are more likely to react appropriately and respect your wishes. You can use this experience to learn, praise yourself for what you did well, and look for ways to improve before tackling more challenging family members.

Phrases to practice:

- I/we want you to feel confident in your decisions, but I would like you to respect my opinions.

- I/we will not tolerate any activity that breaks the law.

- It's important to us that you live by our rules, but we still value your opinion.

- I/we respect that your room is your space, but you need to respect our joint efforts to keep our home clean.

———

Practicing Boundaries With Different Family Members

Choose a family member with whom you need to establish a boundary, but with whom you also have a close relationship.

This is a family member who will give you a little push back when you set your boundary, but not necessarily so much that it will hurt or cause you excessive stress.

These people value you, and will understand the importance of your needs. They're the perfect family members to talk to about the boundaries you wish to set in general, as well as with them specifically.

Take advantage of these relationships to help you not only establish your first boundaries, but also to talk through and practice with.

CHAPTER 7: 10 GRACEFUL TACTICS TO SET BOUNDARIES WITH PARENTS

Most of us have so much to be thankful to our parents for. They brought us into the world, protected us, put clothes on our backs and food in our stomachs. They have probably lent us their car, money, and a shoulder to cry on.

There are some parents who just love to bring this up at any possible opportunity, whether that's to guilt us into doing something we don't want to, or to dissuade us from doing something that we do.

Who has ever heard something like, "30 hours of labor just to have a son who abandons his mother," or, "I didn't raise you to be selfish."? Both statements may well be true, but they shouldn't be used to manipulate you.

If you're having problems with any of the following parental boundaries, we're going to work through 10 tactics that are graceful, but will firmly get your message across.

- Suffocating love

- Codependency

- Interfering with your personal life

- Too opinionated regarding your love life

- Unsolicited advice on your parenting style

- Obsessive purchasing of things for your home (or children)

- Unnecessary or hurtful comments on your body, image, clothes, etc.

- Turning up unexpected

- Constantly disagreeing with your views

- Planning your schedule or free time

As older people, parents are often stuck in their ways. You might find that they're also from a generation of authoritarian parents, where there was no other choice but to listen to and obey the rules of the parents. If your parents never set boundaries with their parents, it could be harder for you.

Also, many times, parents are completely unaware that their actions are upsetting you. By now you have probably tried having a conversation, but your parents continue to break your boundaries. I know that I used to get angry with my parents, and this would only make me feel guilty afterward.

Whatever your emotions were in the past, don't assume that

the same will happen this time. Just because they're your parents, it doesn't mean you should give up on your boundaries and accept that this is how life is going to be.

Why Are Boundaries With Parents More Complex?

In the first place, it is down to the way we feel about our parents and what our relationship should be like with them. They've probably made a lot of sacrifices for us, and to an extent, we feel like we owe them for this.

The other major issue is that parents find it almost impossible to let go of their control. From your parents' point of view, you are, and always will be their child.. You are an extension of their own lives.

Some parents don't want you to make the same mistakes as they did, and others may have missed out on opportunities and are trying to relive their life through yours. All of this creates a very controlling environment.

As the child, we assume that things will change when we turn 18 or move into our own place. Oftentimes, our relationships with parents can take an even more negative turn because this fear of losing control causes them to try to control us even more. It is this need to control that leads parents to overstep boundaries continuously.

This attempted control can be very obvious as they repeatedly tell you what to do or how to do it. You can spot this because they will have quite dominating words and body language.

It could also be more manipulative: making you feel as if

they need you to be able to survive is a form of playing on your kindness and generosity.

Finally, they can use silence as a form of control. Purposely creating space, not contacting you, or ignoring your calls and messages is a psychological game designed to make you come running to them.

There is a gigantic spectrum when it comes to dealing with challenging parents. One person might not be able to cope with a mother who is constantly asking them questions.

The pressure can be so much that they turn to drinking and drugs as a form of escape. Others won't see this as a huge cause for concern because they have to deal with verbally and physically abusive parents, even well into adulthood.

It's okay to love your parents despite their control. It's normal to have a love-hate relationship, and in some circumstances, it is okay to hate your parents.

What's most important right now is that you do what you feel is right for your own situation. Nobody but you knows how you feel, what boundaries you want to set, or the type of relationship you hope to get out of it.

You're in a vicious cycle of control, and it is up to you to break it. Once the control is broken, the boundaries become clearer for both parties.

10 Techniques to Assert Boundaries With Your Parents

Our focus now is going to be on 10 things you can do to

enforce boundaries. Just remember that you have to adapt them to match your needs and goals.

1. Break the Control

It's pointless trying to establish boundaries with your parents when they still have the control (Karuna, 2020). Any attempts you make will be met with ridicule, anger, temper tantrums, or just the word "no." They will continue to manipulate you and use your emotions to get what they want.

To break the cycle of control, you first have to be in the right place: a good place. You need to be aware of your emotions, and know how to manage them in all types of situations. You might not be as confident or as strong as you want to be just yet, but you know you're going in the right direction.

Whatever your parents throw in your direction, you need to be able to handle it. This is critical because as soon as you react, whether that is floods of tears or anger, you're putting yourself back into the cycle of control.

Don't be surprised if this causes parents to push further or up their game. It's going to be a shock for them not to experience the same reaction as normal.

You might hear hurtful insults, like, "You're selfish," or "You're ungrateful." They could try to regain control by reminding you that they're the parent, and you're "just" the child. They may even kick you out.

The harsh lesson of "realizing how lucky you were to have

parents that cared for you" might come up, which is another reason why you have to be prepared for any outcome. The truth is, they are only creating this space in the hope that you will return to your placid people-pleasing self.

Keep telling yourself that you aren't a child anymore, and that you are an independent human being who deserves respect from everyone, including your parents.

If it gets to a point where you can't cope with your parents' reaction, you must walk away. You aren't abandoning them or running away from your problems. You're protecting yourself.

You may have to go for a walk, or you may have to stay with a friend for a while. It could take a couple of weeks. Have faith in your own instincts because you will know when the time is right.

Phrases that will help you to break the control cycle include:

• I won't allow you to use guilt to control me.

• My feelings are as equally important as yours.

• As an adult, I'm no longer scared of you.

• If you choose to ignore me or not love me, that's your issue, not mine.

2. Start With a Conversation

Now that the control cycle has been broken, the dynamics of your relationship will have changed. Contact your parents, and let them know that you would like to talk to them about a few things.

Choose the right time: a time when you're mentally and physically strong, and when you don't have a ton of other things on your mind that could impact your stress levels.

Knowing that they don't have the same control over you, your parents might have seen a side of you that they hadn't before. Hopefully, they will now see you as the adult you have become, and treat you as such. For some families, this break in control is all that's needed for boundaries to be discussed, and together, agreed upon.

For example, if you're comfortable with them having a key to your home, you can agree to give them one, but on the condition that they message or call the day before and don't just show up.

For parents who are all over your love life, you can let them know that they can show interest and ask questions, but they can't keep trying to set you up with every single person they know.

To start your conversation, you can try sentences like:

- I would like to have a conversation with you about my feelings.

- It would be nice if we could sit down and talk about things without getting angry or upset.

- I want to talk to you about this, but I won't stay if I feel threatened.

- It is not that I want to create distance between us. I just want you to understand that there are some areas of my life I don't want to talk about.

3. Empathize With Your Parents

This is incredibly hard, particularly if they have driven you to a point of anxiety or depression. If you're able to see things from their point of view, it will be easier for you to understand their behavior.

A great example is a single parent who projects their fears onto you and your relationship. If your dad was cheated on and he categorizes your girlfriend as "all women," it can be very hurtful. Being able to imagine the pain he went through and his fear that the same thing will happen to you can help you to understand his actions.

A lot of interfering in your life could come down to a parent's fear of being alone. When parents reach a certain age (often closely linked to retirement age) they have an enormous amount of free time that they aren't used to. It has been known for moms to go to their adult child's home and clean, or even do the laundry. Dad might pop round to fix up those DIY jobs that have been on your to-do list.

This sounds quite heavenly for a busy person, but it isn't just a step over a boundary – it is a leap into your personal space. Yet the only reason they've done it is that they wanted to help, and their lives were a little empty.

This is not to say that empathizing is the same as accepting or permitting. You still need to have a conversation about the correct boundaries. However, if you can approach the conversation having thought about their intentions, your words will be kinder.

There is a fine line between being empathetic and appearing weak.

Below are some phrases that meet the balance:

• I can see that you're worried about me, but I know that I've thought about it from every perspective.

• I understand that you're angry, but you can talk to me instead of shouting at me.

• If we just talk about it, you'll see that I agree with you, but I want to do it my own way.

• I need you to respect the fact that after a hectic week, I have to have some time to disconnect.

4. Teach Your Parents; Don't Do It for Them

This one often goes unmentioned with parents, but it's becoming a growing concern, especially with new technology.

I learned very quickly that if I popped over to my parents' house to fix something, they would have no issues calling me for every tiny problem they couldn't resolve.

Alexa was talking to the TV, the printer was jammed, the kitchen sink was leaking, the dog was chewing its tail, and so on.

It started small, but it got to the point where I couldn't make plans because I was expecting my daily call to solve a problem they could find the answer to online.

I love the proverb, "Give a man a fish and you feed him for a day; teach a man to fish and you feed him for life."

In my case, if I taught my parents how to fix their own issues, they wouldn't feel as if they needed me. The times that I did then go to visit were much more enjoyable.

Some skills you aren't going to be able to teach. If your parents don't drive and they have errands to do, of course, you should help. Just make sure that you're arranging a time to help them that suits you.

It's important that you tell your parents that you're going to show them how to do things. For example:

- I'll come over to show you so that you're able to do it yourself next time.

- I can explain to you over the phone, or I can come over to explain, but not until the weekend.

- Have you tried to do it yourself?

- I'll send you a video that shows you how to do it.

5. Set Consequences for Your Parents' Behavior

Yes, parents need consequences too. Let's say you broke the control cycle and had a meaningful conversation about how your mom resorts to crying every time you assert yourself. She promised not to do it again, and for a while, you could see the effort she was making. But then there came a time when the tears started again.

This is perfectly normal because to maintain boundaries, you need to keep working on them. If reminding your mom isn't working, you need to explain what will happen if her actions continue.

You don't want to come off as condescending or as if you're treating her as the child in the relationship.

You should also keep in mind that the attention should be on how you're feeling – "Mom, I'm emotionally drained, and I can't cope with you crying when it isn't necessary. If I say no to you, it's not because I don't love you; it's because I need to take care of myself. If you can't see this, I won't be able to visit as often, and I don't want that."

Alternatively, if you feel you need to be firmer, you could say something along the lines of, "Mom, we've discussed this. I'm not going to keep visiting if you can't respect my boundaries."

What's equally important as establishing boundaries with your parents is to follow through with the consequences. Empty promises will only encourage parents to cross other lines. With this in mind, never explain a consequence without being fully confident that you can go through with it.

A healthy boundary is to only let your parents buy your children sweets once a week. If you have to enforce a consequence like only being able to see the grandchildren once a week because they don't listen, you can't then call them up and ask them to look after your kids. You need to be able to stick to the once-a-week consequence.

Aside from the sentences we have seen, consequences might look like this:

- When you don't respect how I raise my children, I feel it's best not to bring them to visit.

- I don't have to listen to you insult me. If you can't speak to me calmly, I'll come back another day.

- I'll come to the lunches that I can. If you keep insisting that I come to all of them, I won't come to any.

- I love you, but if you can't say anything nice about my relationship, I don't want to talk about it at all.

6. Don't Feel Like You Have to Do This Alone

Establishing boundaries with your parents isn't a competition, but you can feel slightly outnumbered if you're planning to have a conversation with two people on your own.

If you've tried to have these necessary conversations and they didn't go as planned, you can't give up. First, take some time to practice exactly what you want to say with a friend or an understanding relative. Ask them to be very honest and provide you with their feedback, not just on how you present your boundary, but also on other aspects of your communication, such as your tone of voice and body language.

Even with practice and confidence beforehand, the idea of trying to express the boundaries again can bring up fear and anxiety.

Ask a person you trust to come with you for support. It

won't be their task to have the conversation, but just knowing that someone is there next to you can help to keep you calm and confident, and also prevent the situation from spiraling out of control.

7. Respect Your Parents' Values, Beliefs, Culture and Opinions

Your parents are the source of the problem, so don't feel guilty or put the blame on yourself. Nevertheless, it doesn't hurt to see if there are things you can do to ease particular situations.

Politics and religion are two examples where we have to tread carefully, as even though your parents raised you, as an adult, you may have developed your own views. These are also two topics that people can often feel very passionate about.

Part of the controlling behavior from parents is going to follow through into your religious and political views, from how you choose to raise your child and the diet that you want to try, to pretty much anything that goes against their traditional beliefs.

As an adult and a human being, you're entitled to your own opinions. You might be well-read on a subject or have no interest in it at all, but you have the right to express this, just as they do. Modeling behavior is one way that you can educate your parents on beliefs, especially if they continue to disrespect boundaries that you've set.

Generally speaking, in my family, we avoid talking about politics because of our strong opinions. I was so shocked when one year, my mother-in-law at the time asked me who I had voted for, and then told me that she hoped it was her party because they were obviously the best. I didn't agree with her, but I was so blown away that I couldn't answer. Her continuous asking eventually led me to explain that in my family, we don't talk about politics. I could see that this wasn't an acceptable answer for her, and she looked at me as if I were the one in the wrong or I just didn't know anything about politics. I had to remember that this was her problem, not mine.

When parents bring up topics that you don't want to talk about, simply say, "I don't talk about topics like this." Full stop! You don't need to explain why. You can also use phrases like, "I can see your point of view and I respect that, but as you aren't willing to accept that I have my own opinions, I won't talk about the subject." Naturally, it won't be the last time your parents bring up a subject that you won't agree on.

Stand your ground, and keep repeating that you aren't going to get into a debate about something you both feel strongly about. You might also have to set a consequence if they continue to upset you.

When it comes to our values, we often feel even more strongly about them. Two lines I will not allow people to cross are racism and (this probably sounds strange to some) speaking ill of the dead.

Ironically, these are values I share with my mom, but my dad will cross the line. My mom puts up with it, and I used to. I have clearly expressed this boundary, and I've said that

I won't tolerate it. If my dad crosses the line, I stand up, give them both a kiss, and say goodbye. Then I remove myself from the situation that's upsetting me.

Cultural differences can be extremely challenging, but that's not to say that you don't have the right to establish your boundaries as you see fit. For those who come from a culture where close relationships and intrusive behavior are part of the norm, it's hard to see your friends enjoy a more relaxed and less controlling relationship with their parents.

The one things you should avoid saying are things like, "All my friends..." because your parents will come back with the all-time classic, "If all your friends jumped off a bridge, would you jump?"

Instead, use sentences that remind them that you aren't abandoning your culture and you completely respect where they're coming from, but that you need to find a middle ground that includes aspects from your culture and the new one you're living in.

More ideas for phrases would be:

● I know you favor this political party and I respect that, but you need to respect that I have a different opinion.

● Our culture is very important to me too. I'm not abandoning it; I'm finding my own way.

● I don't feel comfortable discussing this as we have different beliefs.

● I will gladly listen to your opinion if you're willing to listen to mine.

8. How to Deal With Parents Who Insult Your Choices

Do you have parents who hate your partner, your job, your house, or your hair? Do they complain that your clothes aren't right? It's a cruel world, and unfortunately, some people are used to listening to their parents calling them fat, ugly or stupid. This doesn't always represent the entire relationship.

Together, you could have other times that are great, but the times it gets dark are extremely painful, and something nobody should have to deal with.

There is only truth in their words if you choose to believe them. I've had moments when I've felt overweight and known I needed to do something about it. There have been other times when someone has said, "Look at the tummy on you!" when I was actually feeling better about myself. You're not stupid, and nobody is ugly because it should only matter what's on the inside.

There are some important facts to remember when dealing with cruel parents:

1. They are unlikely to change, and you can't fix their issues.

2. Their insults are a sign of their own emotional immaturity.

3. It's unlikely you will ever gain their approval.

4. This is emotional abuse.

Emotional abuse takes many forms aside from insults.

They might give you the silent treatment, threaten you, withhold their love or affection, set unreasonable expectations, play mind games, check your phone or computer, or isolate you from people you love. Some emotionally abusive parents think it's okay to belittle your achievements or highlight your mistakes.

If you've tried to implement boundaries and your parents aren't making any effort to change, or you've reached the point where you mentally can't take any more, it's time to step away and limit the contact as much as possible.

If you aren't ready for a complete cut off, keep your interactions short.

If you're still living at home, this is more of a challenge. Find friends and other family members who you can spend time with, and when you're at home, try to limit the time you have with them.

After this much time with an abusive parent, you have probably discovered that there are certain triggers that cause your parents to hurt you.

And no, you are not a trigger, and triggers aren't excuses for behavior. Alcohol, drugs, or an abusive partner are examples of what may trigger your parents' abuse. It is a good idea to look out for these triggers so you can avoid the aftermath.

As hurt as you feel, you need to be the emotionally mature person in the relationship.

Rather than fighting back, choose from the short phrases below to end the conversation:

- That really hurt.

- You're allowed your opinion.

- It's a shame you feel that way.

- Please stop insulting me.

- No, I'm not going to do that.

- Thank you for letting me know that.

- Your opinion doesn't interest me.

- Goodbye.

Walking away from this horrible treatment is the healthiest thing for you to do. Whether you feel that you need to be alone or with someone you trust, take some time to process your emotions instead of bottling them up. Talk to other people, or keep a journal. Use the deep breathing techniques we've worked on, or use a guided meditation video. Don't get trapped in a place where you're hurting. Revisit your goals, and make plans that are going to make for a better future.

9. Try the Loving Approach

This is not going to work in every case of controlling parents. Firstly, you might not feel like you're capable of showering your controlling parent with love. Secondly, they just might be too wrapped up in their own feelings and needs to appreciate the step you are taking.

The loving approach could work for those parents who don't have enough going on in their own lives to keep themselves busy, or who are feeling lonely with their empty nest. They might just require enough reassurance that they've done an amazing job raising you, and that you're still going to be there for them and love them, even if you do have to say no or if they can't keep up their smothering love.

Kind words and kind actions can not only reassure a parent who feels they're losing control, but they can also open up the door to a closer and more loving relationship.

When it comes to narcissistic, codependent, and toxic or abusive parents, it's still worth trying the loving approach. It could be a way to break down the incredibly hard wall they've built up around them. However, in more cases than not, this reassures you that you've tried absolutely everything to develop a healthy relationship with your parents.

10. When It's Time to Walk Away

Sometimes, words and consequences are not going to have the impact we had hoped for. This is most often going to be the case with toxic, abusive and/or codependent parents. You may feel that you've tried everything possible and your parents are still treating you in a way you can't cope with. Let's look at what constitutes everything possible:

• You've taken a very long hard look in the mirror and decided the changes you want to make.

• You've had an open conversation about the boundaries

you wish to implement, using kind words and sentences that emphasize your feelings rather than their behavior.

● If your parents react badly to your boundaries or continue to disrespect them, you have used firmer vocabulary and introduced consequences.

● When your parents still don't respect your words, you follow through on your consequences.

● You've asked a friend or family member to support you while you explain the boundaries and stricter consequences.

● You've asked for professional help, but you still feel like there's no progress.

After so many attempts, and probably months of effort, your parents are obviously not going to appreciate that you're an independent adult who's capable of making their own way in life.

This is a very individual decision depending on the situation, but for your own welfare, it might be time to walk away. When we talk about walking away, it could be for a few weeks, a few months, or more permanently. It might mean that you walk away and only have limited contact when you decide so that there's still an element of contact. Or it may be that you have to leave this relationship behind completely.

It's a heart-breaking decision for lots of people, but there also comes a huge sense of freedom when the decision is made. The pressure of trying to please impossible people, the fear of abuse, and the constant demands just disappear, and all of a sudden, your life becomes your own.

The fact that you have had the strength to say no once and for all will give you the confidence and power to create balanced, fulfilling relationships with people who love you for who you are.

It's also possible that this separation causes your parents to change their behavior. They might get the help they need and reach out to you. This opportunity to restart the relationship is going to be up to you, but take it slowly and with caution. Take the time to see that they're genuine before opening your heart up to being hurt again.

If you feel that some professional help is necessary but you aren't sure where to turn, you can have a look at HAVOCA (Help for Adult Victims of Child Abuse). The site has a forum, support group, and the chance to find a suitable therapist, as well as some amazing resources.

Some parents will learn very quickly that you're determined to maintain your boundaries. Others will test the limits you have in place in the hope they're able to find your weak spot and regain their control, which is why persistence and determination are critical.

If you're someone who has to break away from their parents, don't feel guilty or regret your decisions. You haven't made them lightly, so have faith that you made the right ones.

As your life starts to quickly fill up with happiness, the pain will fade.

———

Practice Setting Boundaries With Your Parents

Take a few minutes to think about how you would respond to your parents in these situations:

1) Your parents turn up at your house at 9am on a Saturday morning with plans for your day.

2) Your mom insists you come over to pick up a curry she's made you, but you're going out for dinner.

3) Your parents go absolutely silent when you express your boundaries. All you get are some grunts and huffs.

4) Your dad mocks you in front of everyone at family gatherings.

CHAPTER 8: BOUNDARIES WITH YOUR PARTNER

W e start each new romantic relationship wide-eyed, eager and positive. We learn from our past mistakes, and as we mature, we feel more comfortable that this is the right person. At first, the relationship blossoms, and it seems like nothing could go wrong. We call this the honeymoon period.

Life starts to throw the usual challenges at us, stress rears its ugly head, and we start to show and see sides of us that were dormant during the honeymoon phase. You might have the first argument or just start to doubt your original positivity.

As problems escalate, it's hard to tell if the problems are things that can be fixed or if this is how life is going to be. Ending a relationship, even a bad one, is never easy, and can cause you to feel like a failure, so sometimes we put up with certain behavior because it's easier.

However, there comes a point when the relationship

becomes so toxic that your life becomes depressing, your partner expects too much from you, and you wake up each day just to go through the motions.

Boundaries within a romantic relationship are probably some of the most important to establish in your life. Your partner is the person who you likely spend the most amount of time with – you could live with them or even work with them. They may know things about you that nobody else does, despite not having known you for as long as your family members have.

As with boundaries and our family members, there's a wide spectrum with regards to the need for boundaries. There could be niggly things that cause arguments or more severe issues such as narcissism, codependency, and abuse. We will look at the dynamics of these relationships separately, as well as examples of how couples have managed to set their healthy boundaries.

Before working on boundaries, it's necessary to have a check of your own mental health to ensure you're not confusing other issues with the need for boundaries.

What Does a Healthy Romantic Relationship Look Like?

Each person you ask will give you a different answer to this question. Some will say it's trust, others a sense of humor. It's possible that you feel physical intimacy is more important, while others need space. All of these are very true. But there are still key aspects that make for a healthy relationship.

Inter-dependent is an excellent description of a good relationship: it is one where you depend on each other for support, but you are strong enough to remain an individual. So, as an example, you have plans together, but you're still able to do things alone if necessary. You can meet with your friends and have your own hobbies, which relates to time apart and personal space.

Healthy relationships make you feel like you're a part of a team. You can learn new things from each other and take an interest in each other's hobbies and goals. You may even be able to support your partner in achieving their goals without taking over. Arguments will come up, but together, you need to have the communication skills to resolve them.

Naturally, intimacy is a large part of a healthy relationship, but that doesn't mean that you need to have the same (often unrealistic) passion we see in the movies. Aside from the sexual boundaries we discussed in Chapter 1, intimacy will include hugs, kisses, cuddles and handholding.

Why Is Your Mental Health Important?

In 2012, a study was carried out on couples in those first stages of love. They displayed significantly higher levels of oxytocin than in those who were single. This rush increases relaxation, our ability to communicate positively, trust, empathy, and psychological stability.

Meeting a new partner and enjoying those first stages of a new romance makes us feels like we've been fixed, often mentally and physically.

So, what happens when the real world comes crashing back down to reality?

We soon realize that our own mental problems are still present, and will have an impact on the relationship.

Stress, anxiety and depression will cause you to see things in a different way. It's so much harder to enjoy time together when all you want to do is be alone. After a time, your partner may struggle with your mental issues, and this can create tension in the relationship.

We've spent some time looking at how to create boundaries with codependents, but you might be the person with codependent issues. This is not your fault: it may be due to problems from your childhood or past relationships. If you're the type of person who is needy or starts to rely on a partner for their own happiness, you may end up suffocating your partner.

Mental health problems are nothing to be ashamed of or anything to hide. Johns Hopkins estimates that 26% of Americans over the age of 18 suffer from a diagnosable mental disorder annually (Johns Hopkins, 2021).

Many mental health disorders are diagnoses that do not go away, and we have to learn how to deal with them before expecting another person to be able to understand the disorder. It is essential that you know who you are, and you are able to love yourself for who you are.

If you know you're in a good place mentally and physically but still feel that the issues in your relationship could be greatly reduced with boundaries, don't worry: we're going to dive deeper into various problematic relationships and what can be done.

Relationship Type #1 - New Relationships

Those first few weeks and months of a new relationship are essential for setting the tone for a long-lasting and happy relationship. As we've mentioned before, it's also a trickier time because of the flood of love hormones.

It's common to feel that boundaries aren't necessary because everything's perfect. It's actually these moments that lay the foundations for the future.

While you're tempted to change your behavior to please the other person, in many cases, the other person will be doing the same, and to an extent, that's nice.

It's good to be open to new concepts and experiences, but there has to be a limit. If there isn't, you'll find that lots of small changes soon lead to looking in the mirror and not recognizing who you are.

If you're unfortunate enough to be dating a narcissist, allowing boundaries to be crossed at this stage makes it easy for them to find your weak spots and then play on them.

Just because you want to establish boundaries in a new relationship, it doesn't mean that you're boring or that you aren't a good partner.

Let's take, for example, a new partner who sends too many messages or calls you constantly. You can put this down to excitement, but there will come a point when it becomes too much.

You might start to feel suffocated, or that you can't do anything without your partner checking in. The excitement of those messages soon becomes dread as you feel like you're being controlled.

It would be healthier for you to establish a boundary in the first moment that the excessive contact starts to upset you.

You can start with a simple message like, "I love your texts, but I'm busy right now. Talk later!" –and don't forget to add your kisses or usual emoji so they don't read in emotions that aren't there.

If the behavior continues, you might need to be firmer: "I can't talk – I'm working."

If you feel that a text isn't enough for them to refrain from the continuous messaging, you will have to have, at first, a light-hearted conversation.

Again, remind them that while you love hearing from them, you're often not in a position to be able to reply.

You need to focus on your work, or that you need time to be with your friends or family. You could talk about times that are convenient for both of you to text or call.

Don't forget that a consequence might have to be put in place. Letting someone know that you can't be in a relationship with someone who can't respect a communication boundary isn't a threat: it is honesty.

As a general rule in new relationships, it's often not until a boundary issue arises that you become aware of it.

A new person in your life is allowed to express their likes

and dislikes regarding how you dress, or even your opinions. But they don't have the right to expect you to change for them.

Seriously consider what your limit is, and deal with it straight away. It's easier to enforce a boundary earlier than to leave it for later down the road. Not only that, but you also increase the chances of the relationship thriving.

Here are some examples of boundaries to communicate in a new relationship:

- I don't like it when people abbreviate in text messages.

- I'm happy to try new things, but I won't have them forced on me.

- I'm not necessarily looking for long-term commitment, but I'm happy to see where things go.

- I need one hour a week to be alone and catch up on my favorite series.

Relationship Type #2 - Established Relationships

If you've been in a relationship for a while, you probably feel quite comfortable around your partner, and you know the good and bad sides of each other. Still, if you weren't able to implement boundaries early on, there will probably be things that your partner does that irritate, frustrate or upset you.

You may have recently moved in with each other, and seen a side to them that you hadn't seen before. Even life-changing events like births, moving house, or the death of a loved one can add stress, sometimes leading to problems that last longer than expected.

The fear of not being liked may have subsided, but only to be replaced by the fear of someone leaving you. If you've tried to express your boundaries previously, it might have caused an argument, and now you may think that it's not worth bringing up the subject again. Falling into this way of thinking only leads to a miserable relationship and life for you. You may even start to resent the other person – and yourself for not standing up for yourself.

As with all boundary-setting, the first stage is to be exceptionally clear about the boundaries you wish to create and where there is room for negotiation. If your partner constantly complains because you work overtime, do they have a point?

Try to see things from both perspectives because sometimes in a long-term relationship, we want to create a boundary that we think we need but isn't necessarily good for us. You're working overtime so that you can save for a new home together.

Your partner complains, not because they're jealous of the time you spend at work or the fact that you aren't home. It might be expressed the wrong way, but they're just genuinely concerned for you. If you go back to check your communication skills, some of the problems can be resolved with an open conversation.

How you start the conversation is crucial for setting the right tone. Regardless of your gender, when you hear the words, "We need to talk," after a long day, you're just drowned by a feeling of dread, and possibly even annoyance. The word "boundaries" can also stir up negative ideas about what's to come.

Remember that just because you know what you want to say, it doesn't mean that the other person is ready to listen. Make sure that neither of you is tired, and that the atmosphere is positive. There shouldn't be any other underlying problems that can be dragged up in a new conversation.

In order to not turn a conversation into an argument, you need to keep your sentences focused on your emotions rather than the actions of your partner.

There is quite a difference between, "You make me so angry when you complain about my overtime," and, "I feel angry when you complain about my overtime." The first sentence implies that they are the cause of your emotions, while the second shows that you're taking responsibility for your feelings rather than blaming your partner.

After you have expressed the behavior you want to change, wait for a response, and actively listen. You should always have a backup conversation if your partner is unable to see or understand the boundary you're trying to establish. But that doesn't mean that it's the only direction the conversation will take.

Listening to what your partner says rather than assuming you know what they will say is how the boundary will be fully accepted. If your partner explains that they're worried about your health, you can decide on a time limit for your overtime. If your partner is upset because there's nobody home to cook dinner, then you can see that they're more concerned about their needs than your wellbeing.

It's important that you control any anger that may arise, and explain that resolving financial issues is more important than who will cook the dinner. If you're willing, you could suggest that one or two nights a week, you will finish early to cook if they can stop complaining.

This is only one of numerous examples in a well-established relationship. A bugbear for so many couples is the housework. Your partner might be more than happy to let dishes pile up or leave clothes all over the floor.

Remember that every time you do the dishes, pick up the clothes, or do anything that you don't want to do, you're teaching your partner that it is okay for them to act in this way.

Creating new boundaries after so much time together isn't unnecessary, and it's not necessarily a sign of deeper issues. It's normal to fall into a routine when things become assumed instead of spoken.

To make boundaries easier, keep working on your communication. Why not try some of these ideas:

- I need time to spend with my friends, as do you.

- I feel like I'm being treated like the cleaner rather than your partner.

- My career is just as important as yours.

- I'd like there to be more balance between the time we spend with your family and the time we spend with mine.

Relationship Type #3 - The Codependent Partner

There are two sides to codependency, and they are related. Someone who is codependent might have issues with addiction, whether that's drugs, alcohol, work or sex.

A codependent partner is someone who relies on the validation and emotions of others. Codependency in women is widely talked about. We need to be careful because men are just as likely to become codependent, and less likely to discuss it (Lancer, 2020). Many use addiction as a means of escapism or as something they see that they control.

For example, a codependent man might use an addiction to work as a form of providing for his family. The hope is that his partner and children are taken care of, and this way, his family won't leave him. This example doesn't seem too painful, but in reality, his work is a cover for identifying the real needs of his family.

Similarly, drug and alcohol abuse allow people a break from stress and anxiety, but the problems are still very much there.

Addiction is rarely a problem that you can overcome alone. If your partner is an addict, valiant as it may be, it isn't healthy for you to be the solution. Part of sobriety and recovery is to gain self-esteem, a feeling that you have this ability to control your habit yourself. If your partner needs you to be sober or clean, the codependency deepens.

Please, if your partner has an addiction of any kind, talk to them about it and encourage them to seek professional help. You can lead a horse to water, but you can't make it drink. Provide leaflets and contact information, but it is up to them to take the first step.

On the other hand, codependency doesn't have to stem from addiction (Glass, 2020). A lot of people will say that their partner is too needy, which is the polite way of saying they're codependent. This could look like a person who always seeks your approval. They might struggle to spend time without you, and will not actively make plans alone, but instead, wait to see what you're doing and 'tag along'.

Codependency can cause jealousy, and even violence. You may start to change the way you dress before you go out, or just give up on the idea of going out at all. Jealousy isn't limited to friends. Codependent partners can become jealous of colleagues, and even family.

The first thing to remember is that codependency isn't your fault or your partner's. There is often childhood trauma that leads a person to become dependent on others. In some cases, professional help will be needed, especially if you've tried establishing boundaries and your partner won't accept them.

The second step is to decide what's important for you. What are your hobbies and goals? Where do you see yourself in 6 months or a year?

Don't feel selfish about creating plans for your future. Next, discuss these plans with your partner. You may want to avoid the word "boundaries" as they could see this as a harsh way of trying to create distance between you. Instead, lead by example. Show them how excited you are about your goals, and encourage them to do the same. Help them to discover hobbies and interests that they'd like to do individually. Also, find interests or make plans for things to do together.

You will need to learn how to say no to your codependent partner. You can use the gentle phrases we have practiced like, "It sounds lovely, but I can't," or the firmer approach of, "No, not today." Remember that "yes" and "no" are just words. There are no feelings attached to these words unless you express them in such a way.

If your no is loud and harsh, it sounds angry, but when you say the right way, it can sound loving. It will be a gradual process, and your partner will need to rebuild their confidence so that they're able to do things without you, therefore, giving you the time you need for yourself.

Use these sentences as you create boundaries with a codependent partner:

- I understand that you need help, but I'm too busy today.

- I feel it's healthier if we do this activity separately, and then we can do this activity together.

- I'm going to take some time for myself this weekend to focus on my goals.

- I don't like it when you're jealous. I've never given you a reason to not trust me.

Relationship Type #4 - You Are the Codependent

Codependency and empathy are also closely related.

Codependency could also mean taking on a large part of other people's emotions and feeling responsible for them.

It is impossible to say no, as you can't stand letting your partner down. This goes back to the need to be wanted, needed and loved. There is a heart-breaking reality here.

Do you love the person, or do you love that they need you? If you came home and the laundry was done, the kids were fed, and your dinner was on the table, would you feel happy, or would you feel disappointed?

Being codependent doesn't mean that you can't have a healthy relationship. It just means that rather than trying to fix others, you need to work on fixing yourself. This might include getting help for substance abuse or mental health issues. You might need to focus on your diet, and start looking at hobbies, interests and goals.

Get to know what your triggers are. You might accept emotional or verbal abuse because it's something that was considered normal in your family when you were growing up. Taking care of a family is ongoing.

Have you ever noticed that you can't sit still and read a book because you feel that there's always something you should be doing?

In this case, you need to work on taking time for yourself. Start small, just 5 minutes a day for a coffee in the garden or meditation.

Slowly build on this so that you don't start to feel guilty when you want to introduce a new hobby. Keep telling yourself that this crucial time for yourself isn't abandoning those who need you.

Your partner will still need you, but instead, it will be for the right reasons – because you are their best friend and they enjoy spending time with you.

Let's look at some phrases to use if you're codependent:

- I'm working hard to put my needs first.

- I would appreciate your support in this matter.

- I'm going to take some time for myself, but that doesn't mean I don't love you.

- I feel that it's important that you don't take advantage of my kindness.

Relationship Type #5 - The Narcissist

You might think that a narcissist is easy to spot. Traditionally, we see them as the person in the room who has all eyes on them. They need to be showered with attention; they believe they're more important than others and that they're generally better than everyone else in the room.

A narcissist lacks empathy and will not be able to see any need for the boundaries that you wish to foster. That would mean seeing things from your point of view, which they're incapable of. This is what psychologists call a covert narcissist (Clarke, 2020).

A covert narcissist will also see themselves as superior and lack empathy, but their behavior is more subtle. Sadly, many covert narcissists are masters of manipulation.

A covert narcissist:

• Constantly looks for reassurance regarding their skills or achievements

• Will play the victim rather than outright criticize you or blame you

• Can cause you to doubt your own ideas or question your perspectives

• May use the silent treatment to get what they want

• Might allow you to feel like you're 'winning', but the end goal is what they wanted all along

• Have a habit of being late or not showing up to reiterate your lack of importance in their life

Studies from Washington University have shown that narcissists aren't aware of their behavior. One study showed that while a group of narcissists ranked themselves as being more intelligent and more attractive, they were also tougher on themselves with regards to their negative qualities (Kaufman, 2011). Some people firmly believe that everybody has the ability to change. Others feel that the only reason for a narcissist to change would be if they could see the greater good for themselves.

Whether your partner is capable of change or not will be up to you. If you try the following techniques and your relationship doesn't improve, the healthiest thing to do for you is to walk away.

If you're determined to try everything first, let's look at how you can implement new strategies in your relationship.

• Remember who you are

A narcissist will project their own expectations onto you. If they're the best runner, you are unfit. If they work more hours than you, you're lazy. If you struggle with your finances, you're an idiot. None of this is true.

When your partner expresses their opinions, you can tell them that these words hurt you, but as they are unlikely to empathize with this, you're better off using your energy to protect yourself emotionally.

• Focus on your own independence

You may feel like your partner has the ability to drain all of your power and energy from you. Their intimidation prevents you from standing up for yourself.

Turn your focus onto yourself and what you need to start feeling stronger. As your strength grows, so will your confidence, and you will start to feel more independent.

• Be aware of the manipulation

Whether it's in your face (like shaming you in front of your friends) or subtle (like the bottom lip shaking when you say no), stand your ground. No means no.

I know from experience that this is far easier said than done. But I promise that the rush of empowerment you feel after the first no is worth all of the anxiety leading up to it.

• Escape the silent treatment

The whole point of the silent treatment is that you feel left out in the cold and have to go rushing back to them. If they decide to cut off all communication, go out. See a friend or visit relatives. There's nothing more empowering than going to the cinema or out for dinner alone. You get to enjoy a lovely experience, while your partner has to consider the fact that their tactics aren't working.

• Control your emotions

Whether you need to breathe deeply, count to ten, or walk away, never let your partner see that they've got to you. Part of them feeling better about themselves is to make you feel worse about yourself. If the only thing you can bring yourself to say is "Okay," that's fine. It's better than playing into their emotional game.

• Keep control of your own money

Many couples have a joint account. It makes it easier for you to pay bills. But being together doesn't mean you merge into one being.

As you strive to maintain your independence, you need to maintain control over your own money. Have a joint account and pay equal amounts into it to cover your joint expenses, but don't give up your main account.

Don't allow yourself to get into a situation where you don't have the financial resources to leave if you want to.

• Never give up

A narcissist is going to test every single limit you have. They will try to cross your boundaries, and they'll probably continue to make you feel inferior.

You're going to have to be determined not to give up on yourself. That's not to say that you need to put up a shield to block out your emotions.

Learning to listen to what your emotions are telling you is the best way to start your emotional healing and give you the strength to face the consequences of your boundaries. Determination will only take you so far.

If you don't see the changes in your relationship that you want to see, it's time to end it. Deciding to end a toxic relationship isn't giving up on you: it's giving up on the relationship so that you can live the life that you deserve.

For narcissistic relationships, your phrases will need to be firmer:

- My reasons are personal, and I don't have to explain them to you.

- I'm confident in my choices.

- If you aren't going to respect me, I'll walk away.

- No means no.

Relationship Type #6 - The Abusive Partner

First of all, I'm sorry that you're in this place. It's not your fault, and nothing you have done makes you deserve this treatment. Before we go any further, I urge you not to put yourself in any situation where you're in danger. I commend your bravery, but it's not worth your safety.

If your partner is physically abusive, or you're worried that they might turn abusive, don't try to enforce boundaries alone. You can have the conversation in a public place, or make sure that a friend or family member is with you.

Sometimes, a partner suffers from a mental health disorder that causes them to lash out. This isn't an excuse for their abuse. The chances are that you're an empath and completely understand why they're abusive. But you also need to realize that your feelings are valid.

You have the right to be upset when someone hurts you, and you have a right to express this. Burying your feelings is like feeding the ticking bomb inside you with more explosives. You might hear the words, "I'm sorry," and forgive the behavior.

Abuse is only forgivable if your partner is willing to get the help they need and to put the effort into the relationship.

Victims of both verbal and physical abuse are caught in a nasty cycle. The abuser will abuse, and they will say sorry, perhaps telling you it won't happen again or it was the last time. After this, the victim often forgives. For a short time, the abuser will make an effort, but a trigger will cause them to repeat the behavior. Similar to controlling parents, this cycle has to be broken.

As with before, think very carefully about what your limit is. Is it a verbal insult, a physical threat, or physical contact? Remember that physical abuse doesn't have to leave a bruise. Once your boundary is clear in your mind, decide on the consequence of them breaking this boundary. In other relationships, you might be more inclined to be slightly flexible with your boundaries, and even with your consequences.

With abusive partners, there is no room for the same flexibility: this is your mental and physical safety, and possibly even that of your children.

Let's use the example of a partner who verbally abuses you and has raised a hand, but has never actually hit you. You understand that they have their own problems, and are willing to support them while they get professional help.

While their emotional insults hurt you, you can cope for now. The absolute limit is raising their hand to you. If this happens, you'll leave, and there will be no looking back. Tell your partner that you do love them, and that you want the relationship to work, but only if there's mutual respect and care from both sides.

As there is little room for gray, one of three things will happen. Your partner will deny that there's a problem, call you dramatic, and basically show no signs of respecting your boundary, in which case you have to hold your head high and know that you've tried everything you can.

Your partner may agree to get help and things will go well until the point that they violate your boundary. As tempted as you are to give them one more try because they've been working so hard to improve, take care: they're learning that your boundaries can be broken.

The third possibility is that your partner continues with their therapy and/or treatment, while gradually you become stronger and your partner respects you for this. You can work together at establishing and maintaining new boundaries as your relationship grows.

It would be wrong to imply that there is a one-size-fits-all approach to establishing boundaries with your partner when there are so many factors that influence a relationship. In summary, there are certain stages that will apply to all of us. Let's recap on those:

• Know who you are and what you want from the relationship

• Understand that you're entitled to your own space, time, hobbies, interests, goals and friends

• Decide where there's room for give and take and where the absolute no is.

• Don't feel guilt for expressing your boundaries and expecting respect from your partner

• Find the right time to have a conversation when neither of you is tired, stressed, or preoccupied

• Make sure clear communication is your goal, and this includes your own words as well as what your partner has to say

• Accept that sometimes, we all need a little help, and seeking professional help is not a sign of weakness

Remember that it's okay to walk away from a toxic relationship. Don't despair and start to tell yourself that you're doomed to a life of being single. Take time to learn more about yourself, and become stronger and happier so that you have the right foundations to start a new relationship when you're ready and if you want to.

To keep the focus on your feelings rather than aggravating your abuser, try to remember "I" sentences such as:

- I feel scared when you shout at me.

- I feel personally attacked when you insult me.

- I want to feel important and respected in our relationship.

- I will leave if I don't feel safe in our relationship.

———

Practicing Your Boundaries With Your Partner

To identify exactly what your relationship boundaries look like, write five sentences that start with the words, "I'm not comfortable with…" and another five that begin with, "I draw the line at…"

You may find that when you look more closely at your relationship, there will be more. Start with at least five for each, and then be clear about your consequence for every point.

CHAPTER 9: GENUINE WAYS TO SET BOUNDARIES AND SAVE FRIENDSHIPS

We all need friends. It is been proven scientifically. Experts at the University of Exeter explain that, aside from releasing these wonderful happy hormones like oxytocin and dopamine, there are evolutionary reasons why we need friends.

Sociability is in our genes. Humans have evolved in large groups containing both family members and non-family members. Early friends would have been there to protect other humans from predators, or they would have helped each other to find food (Mandel, 2019). These connections are still important to us, but they have evolved as we have.

Today, we might need support when we have an argument with a relative or partner. Spending time with your friends releases happy hormones that allow us to feel good. But what can you do when these friendships are not quite as balanced as you had hoped?

Friendships are different to other relationships in the sense that they aren't blood, and your friends aren't your life partner. Nonetheless, a friendship that doesn't have boundaries will show the same issues as other relationships. Without boundaries, you might experience:

- A lack of empathy

- Inappropriate amounts of sharing

- Disrespecting each other's time

- Disrespecting religion or values and beliefs

- Controlling decisions rather than supporting

- Putting a friend's needs before your own

- Not saying no when you need or want to

- Putting up with behavior that you don't agree with

- Being too physically close or suffocating

- Toxic friendships

There's also a friendship spectrum, encompassing people who you would call acquaintances, others who are part of a regular circle of friends, and those that you can't imagine life without.

How you go about setting these boundaries will depend on the closeness of your relationship.

You might also have a niggly feeling about a friendship, but you can't identify the source of the problem. It might be as simple as identifying why you need to create these boundaries.

Why Would You Need to Set Boundaries With Friends Now?

If you've just met some new people, it's essential that you establish your boundaries straight away so that your relationship doesn't suffer in the future.

For those friends who've been in your life for some time, don't assume that it's too late. Without sounding like a broken record, boundaries are there to enhance friendships and not to push them away. See if any of the following situations ring true for you.

1. You are overwhelmed. Your family could be putting pressure on you, or you have additional work deadlines. Your boss is going on at you, and the last thing you can handle is your friend adding to the pressure.

2. Your life has changed. Certain events in our lives mean we aren't as available as we used to be. This is often seen when we have children, and that Sunday afternoon beer has been replaced with afternoon naps and diapers.

3. You no longer feel that it's acceptable for you to put more into the relationship. Friendships have to be mutually beneficial so you both put in equal amounts and get equal benefits.

4. You can't trust your friend. Whether they've never been particularly trustworthy or they've recently broken your trust, you need to feel safe to share.

5. You can't accept some of their extreme views. We all have that one friend who is a political buff, or perhaps you

have someone whose opinions of illegal immigrants breaks your heart.

6. You can't do anything without your friend asking what you're doing or where you're going. It has come to a point where their keen interest makes it feel like you have another controlling parent.

7. They are in constant contact or don't appreciate your communication style and technique. A quick meme from a friend midday can boost your mood. 100 texts and half an hour phone calls aren't necessarily productive, and can cause feelings of resent.

8. Your friendship has turned nasty. It could be a combination of one or more of the above. They might be picking at your personality, making fun of you, or bullying you. This toxicity can lead to manipulation and other unhealthy friendship traits.

Two Amazing Techniques for Setting Boundaries With Friends

Before we look at some specific cases of friends who break boundaries, I want to look at two techniques that will help you to determine and establish boundaries. Don't forget: you can use these techniques for boundaries with any person in your life, but they're nice to use with friends as a practice.

The Compass

Sarri Gilman shared a unique way in which she created boundaries in her TED conference. You can either draw a small compass on a piece of paper, or you can visualize one on the palm of your hand.

This compass has just two words: "yes" and "no." It goes back to the idea that yes and no are only words, and there are no emotions attached to these words.

When you enforce your boundaries in your friendships, they will react with their feelings, but you have to remember that this is on them. Your compass has no feelings, and its sole purpose is to take care of you.

So you go about your day, and any time a friend asks something of you, you look at your compass and decide if it is yes or no. Remove the emotions, remove the what-ifs and buts – just answer yes or no. Once you have your answer, you can then choose the right words.

It's not uncommon for your compass to get "clouded over". It's not always clear whether it's a yes or a no. We can't blame the compass: it's just an object. Normally this happens when we don't agree with the initial answer.

Imagine your friend wants you to help them move house. You look at your compass, and it says no because the last thing you want to do is spend your one free day shifting boxes.

Then the tiny voice in your head says, "But it's the nice thing to do, and they helped me when my car broke down." But your answer is no, and you should have faith in that. If your compass is only there to care for you, the answer is no because your body and mind need time to disconnect.

That being said, your compass won't provide you with any

details. It doesn't have the ability to see the middle ground. The idea is that it provides you with the initial answer that you can then work on.

In the case of moving house, you could say, "I can help for 2 hours, but then I have to go." Your boundary is clear, so it's crucial that after 2 hours, you go. If you don't, you have ignored your compass and your own wellbeing.

Sell Your Time

This is an excellent technique to help you visualize your limits. Break down your day into 30-minute slots - so logically, in 24 hours, you have 48 slots.

If we're lucky, we can take away 16 slots for sleeping, and most will have to take away around 16 more for work. You have 16 slots left.

Be precise here: do you need a slot for showering? Do you need two slots for dinner? Once you've delegated your slots to everything you need to do on that day, you'll be left with, let's say, seven slots.

You're now left with the things you want to do and the things your friends want you to do. I'm going to take away two slots because I want to go to the gym. My friend wants to have a drink. Okay, I'll sell two slots to my friend. A different friend wants to go to the movies. This will require at least my remaining five slots, and therefore, I have to say no.

As you get better at saying no based on the number of slots you have available, you will soon start to feel like you have more control over your own time and that you have more time for yourself.

This time alone is energizing, and makes the activities that you do with your friends that much more enjoyable.

You can even combine these two techniques. Use your compass to decide if you say yes or no to selling a time slot.

You can even explain your technique to your friends. When a friend hears, "I don't have time," they assume you're exaggerating or just making things up.

If you say, "Sorry, I only have three slots left today," they can see that you've calculated your time precisely.

They may come back and say, "Can I have one slot?" Well, that's something that may work, depending on whether you want to say yes or not.

There are so many potential issues with friends that all require some form of boundary. We're going to look at some of these with examples of how to be firm and fair.

Your friend laughs at your attempt to set boundaries

Within a friendship or a group of friends, you each develop a role that's hard to break free from. You have the joker, the carer, the planner, and so on.

You probably feel like you don't have a role established, and that you're the submissive one who lets others carry out their roles.

The moment you try to form an opinion, the friend or

group is shocked, and find it funny that all of a sudden you have a voice. They may laugh or ridicule you, and this will hurt. While you shouldn't excuse their behavior, consider whether, on some subconscious level, they're fearful of your boundary, as it means they might have to give up part of their role.

The planner is organizing a dinner for the group. You have always said yes to everything, but this time you don't like the location, and suggest somewhere else. You can imagine the shock on their face, and then they reply with a laugh and ridicule your idea. It was probably a good idea, but deep down, they fear that you'll have more good ideas, and that you'll start to take on the role of planner, leaving them feeling redundant.

Setting boundaries doesn't mean that you're no longer an empath. You can still understand the root of your friends' laughter in order to express boundaries in a way that reassures them.

For example, "I know you love planning, and you've always done such a good job. I just think that the atmosphere is better there." This gives your friend some reassurance in their abilities, and tells them that you have a valid opinion.

Here are some other phrases you can try:

- Please don't laugh at me.

- It hurts me when you ridicule my ideas.

- You know that I get upset when you laugh at me, so why do you keep doing it?

- I feel like your joking has crossed a line.

- No, I don't want to do that because you've hurt me by laughing at me.

- Did I miss the joke?

There's a combination of phrases that emphasize your feelings, and others that highlight bad behavior. Which ones you want to use will depend on how you're feeling at the time.

Friends who never pay

Thanks to technology and payment apps, there's little excuse for someone not paying their way anymore. If you're out for dinner and you pay the bill, they should be able to send a transfer for their share. Still, we all know that one person who never seems to open their wallet.

The solution to this problem is rather simple, regardless of if you're better off than they are or vice versa. You work hard for your income. You want to be able to enjoy your time with friends, but should your 40-hour week really enable them to enjoy their lives that little bit more?

The other way to look at it is that you aren't actually helping them to be responsible with their finances if you're constantly paying.

First of all, prepare yourself for a frank conversation with them. They might not even be aware that they're doing it, so avoid subtle digs. "I love our Saturday lunches together, but I need you to start paying for half."

You shouldn't have to feel like you need to justify this, but you might want to explain that things are tight, or that you're saving for something. If your friend takes offense at this or becomes angry, then it's time for the consequence, and that would be to stop meeting them for lunch.

Your friend dominates conversations

Still bearing in mind that everyone is entitled to express their own opinions, conversations among friends have to have balance. If you feel like your friend chooses all of the topics, voices their opinion, and then doesn't bother to listen to you, you're lacking a boundary.

Being a constant listening ear is exhausting and draining. You can feel undervalued and disrespected. A healthy friendship is one where you can both unload when you need to, or you can both share stories from your day.

The irony is, if you've tried to interrupt your friend to get a word in, you've probably been called rude. Never interrupt: it won't achieve your goal.

What you can do is control how you react to the friend's constant chatter. You probably try to show interest in what they're saying in the hope that they will ask you a question.

From now on, we're going to do the opposite. That's not to say that you're going to start rolling your eyes and huffing and puffing. Instead, remain neutral; only respond to things that you feel are important and keep your comments relative.

While this will help to reduce the extended chatter from your friend, it's likely that you'll still need to make it clear that the conversation needs balance. For example:

- I don't feel like I have a chance to voice my opinion.

- I'd like to feel heard.

- It's important to me that I contribute to the conversation.

- I feel shut out when you hog the conversation.

- I don't feel like you care that you never let me speak.

- I feel like there's distance in our friendship because I don't have the chance to talk.

Once your friend is aware of the problem, it's time to introduce the solution. While it might sound dramatic, a code word is an ideal way to remind your friend that they've slipped into talkative mode: a single word that relates to you both that you can say to pause and remind your friend that you need to have your say.

Friends call you mean when you try to establish your boundaries

It's hard enough to overcome your own fear and worries about coming across as selfish. When a friend calls you mean, selfish, unkind, or any other insult, it should reassure you that this is exactly why boundaries are needed.

Secondly, think about what these words actually mean to you. Your friend won't realize that their insults more accurately describe their own behavior, as they can't see the importance of your needs.

Let's look at the word "mean". It means to be cruel or unkind; however, people throw the word around for situations that really are far from cruel.

If you can't pick your friend up or taxi them around because you already have plans with colleagues, wouldn't it be crueler to cancel on your colleagues?

We've probably all had that moment when we've asked a friend to keep their mask on or wanted to be socially distant, only for them to call us mean.

You aren't being mean at all. You're protecting your health. So remind yourself that you're not mean. And selfish? We aren't talking about sharing your chips or a bag of sweets.

Allowing your friends to manipulate you into doing things you don't want to by insulting you will slowly chip away at your health and your happiness. So again, constantly remind yourself that you aren't selfish.

Tell your friends that you won't tolerate insults because they don't get their way. Explain that there are certain things that you can do, and others that you're not willing to do.

You can explain that you can see their point of view, you understand that they need help or want to do things with you, but there's a right way to ask and a wrong way: "Insulting me is not going to encourage me to say yes to you." You can also point out that they wouldn't like it if you treated them in the same way.

Be confident in your words and body language. Make an effort to ensure that you're facing the person and making eye contact.

Your tone doesn't have to be negative or forceful, but it does have to be direct. Avoid the word "sorry" as it isn't you who should be apologizing.

Put it into practice:

- I'm not mean. I'm taking care of myself.

- I've been hurt too many times by your words. I'm going to take a break from our friendship.

- You're negatively impacting my health, and I need some time away from you.

- If you feel so strongly, I don't see a future for our friendship.

The friend who is always late

I have a friend who is always late. I think in 10 years she has been on time once. There is absolutely no malice in this. She's incredibly disorganized, and talks to everyone in her path. As frustrating as it is, she means no harm. She's also from a different culture where they tend to be more laid back about everything. To handle this, I calculate a half hour difference.

On the other hand, I had a friend who was always late because they wanted their entrance to be dramatic. They wanted the whole room to see that they were more important, that their lives were busier than anyone else's, and their responsibilities were more important. Classic narcissism!

For people who are narcissistic and don't respect boundaries, your phrases will likely fall on deaf ears, but that's not to say that you shouldn't have a frank conversation and implement consequences: "I feel that you don't respect the importance of my time when you're constantly late or don't show up. From now on, I won't wait."

It's short and to the point, and clearly explains that you won't stand for the behavior. Of course, to maintain your boundary, you'll have to leave as soon as your friend is late.

Put it into practice:

• If you arrange to meet me at a certain time, you need to stick to it.

• I don't appreciate being left to wait. I feel it's very inconsiderate.

• It takes less than a minute to send a message and let me know of the change of plans.

• My time is just as important as yours.

Learning how to trust in a friendship again

Breaking someone's trust is incredibly hard to fix. Depending on the degree, it may be impossible to completely overcome. Once bitten, twice shy doesn't only apply to existing friendships: the experience stays with you when you make new friends. When it comes to new friendships, be open about your feelings and past issues.

Many people have had problems with a friend gossiping or talking about them behind their back. This becomes a fear that we assume will happen in all other friendships, but you should always give people the benefit of the doubt.

On that note, if you have a friend who likes gossiping to you, it's more than likely that they gossip about you. If a friend starts to talk about others, tell them straight away that you aren't interested, and bring up a new subject.

Also, look for particular patterns in the friendships you create. You might realize that you tend to form friendships with people who are untrustworthy. There will be a reason behind this, and you should explore it in order to break the pattern.

Don't just look at trust issues within your friendships: also look at your relationships with your partner and family members. You may find that talking to a professional will help you to get to the root of your trust issues.

Now, if your issues are because friends have hurt you, you need to make sure they're aware of the depth of your pain.

Let them know that you're not going to be able to trust them again for some time, and that if they want the friendship to last, they will have to prove their trustworthiness.

An amazing quote I once read was, "Trusting you is my decision. Proving me wrong is yours."

It's your choice to trust someone, and it will take time. If the behavior continues, even after several attempts to establish your trust boundaries, the friendship has become unhealthy, and even toxic. These people are doing more harm than good, and you should consider walking away.

Put it into practice:

• I don't gossip, and I don't listen to gossip.

- I'm not comparing you to my past friends, but I've had problems in the past, and I'm learning to trust again.

- I'm incredibly sad about what you've done. I need time to process it.

- I need you to stick to your promises if you want me to trust you again.

The big one - friends who don't respect boundaries

You've taken a look at yourself, and you clearly know what you want from your friendships. You've asked your compass and decided what is a firm yes and what is a firm no, and you've identified the areas that can be negotiated. You've used the right language and short phrases, and you've set the consequences.

Even after reiterating boundaries and following through with the consequences, your friends still try to push the limits.

Imagine you can only have five foods for the rest of your life. Are you going to choose the unhealthy or the healthy?

If you only had room in your world for five friends, would you still hang on to the toxic friendships, or would you be more willing to break the contact knowing that you now have room for friends who have your best interests at heart?

As we grow up, our life circumstances change. We mature, we learn, and we see things from different points of view. Sometimes, our friends do the same, but in opposite directions.

There's no rule that says you have to remain friends with someone no matter what.

Put it into practice:

● I have said no, and I mean no.

● I'm putting my needs first, and you won't make me feel guilty.

● If you can't respect me for who I am, I can't see a future for our relationship.

● I'm very upset by your actions, and I need space from you.

––––––

Initially, setting boundaries will cause you stress, but it's not permanent. Once you've set your boundaries, your friends will respect them, or they won't. You will notice that once you end the friendship, or at least distance yourself from these boundary-breakers, your stress will ease.

There is still one other group of people that we need to form boundaries with. A group of people that we spend the biggest part of our day with – our colleagues. The next chapter is going to be dedicated to those workmates who know exactly what buttons to push to get a reaction.

CHAPTER 10: BOUNDARIES IN THE WORKPLACE FOR A MORE POSITIVE ENVIRONMENT

Hollywood has a habit of romanticizing workplace boundaries. Don't get me wrong, I love a rom-com as much as the next, but they tend to turn very real issues into a humorous situation where inevitably, two boundary breakers fall in love.

Take *Two Weeks' Notice* with Sandra Bullock and Hugh Grant. Grant's character calls his assistant (Bullock) at an inappropriate time for an "emergency": he couldn't choose a tie!

Unfortunately, for many of us, there isn't a Grant or Bullock for us to fall in love with, and we don't have to suffer a negative or even toxic environment day in and day out.

The harsh fact is that we spend approximately half of our waking hours in the workplace. Today, 50-hour weeks are becoming the norm, and even 60-hour weeks aren't uncommon (Business News Daily, 2020).

Problems at work and with colleagues are going to have a knock-on effect in other areas of your life. Workplace stress has a huge impact on employees and employers.

83% of US workers suffer from work-related stress, and a massive 1 million workers miss work each day due to stress. The cost to businesses in the US is up to $300 billion, and $51 billion of this is due to absenteeism caused by depression.

Naturally, there are various reasons for workplace stress. That being said, boundaries could help the 39% of people whose workload causes them stress, and the 35% of people whose boss is the main cause of their stress (The American Institute of Stress, 2019).

When there are no boundaries at work, stress builds up. You wake up in the morning, and you dread starting your day. Tasks are more challenging, colleagues are more annoying, and not even the end of the day makes you any happier.

Many people also have to take work home with them. The constant strain of having to answer the phone, reply to a text, or check emails takes its toll.

Tiredness turns into exhaustion, anxiety, and often mental health issues, physical health issues, and even substance abuse. The lack of strength makes it more difficult to set and maintain boundaries with your friends and family.

What Are Workplace Boundaries?

Workplace boundaries are a set of legal and ethical practices that allow employees to feel safe, both physically and emotionally, in a work environment.

Some workplace boundaries are very clear, especially when they're the law. A relatively new boundary that we must all comply with is around privacy laws. Sexual harassment is now a hot issue, especially since the #MeToo movement. There are others that we still need to consider, as well as people who don't seem to understand how close their actions come to breaking the law.

Workplace boundaries include:

- Bullying

- Racism

- Discrimination

- A narcissistic boss

- Flirting

- Asking personal questions

- Working without pay

- Not using your vacation days

- Working through your breaks

- Taking on other people's responsibilities

- Taking on too big a workload

- Saying yes to jobs you don't have the skills for

An element of common sense will be required. For example, when asking personal questions, if your boss asks you about your family, they might be showing a genuine concern. If a boss starts to ask about your kids' grades, where your partner works, and what you had for breakfast on Saturday, it becomes intrusive. You may also have a tight deadline or a meeting that can't be changed. On this occasion, you don't mind skipping your break.

The need for workplace boundaries will come when the action starts to make you feel uncomfortable or unhappy. If I saw a woman looking at me and smiling, I would take it as a compliment. The next man might find it uncomfortable. The law is clear to a degree, but there is still a gray area that you need to navigate your way round based.

The Benefits of Establishing Boundaries in the Workplace

When you decide to implement boundaries in the workplace, it's not about being right or wrong, nor is it about asserting your dominance. Your boundaries won't make you unpopular or the party pooper of the office. On the contrary:

1. Boundaries allow for a respectful workplace. Not just respect for the superiors, but for people in every position.

2. Employees will be able to clearly see what behavior is considered acceptable in the workplace. Not every location or industry will have the same rules, so boundaries make it easier for people to follow acceptable behavior.

3. Creating boundaries promotes positive communication. When people feel safe to talk about their concerns, you can start to have more open and direct conversations, which is incredibly productive.

4. Not having boundaries makes it harder to discuss and

manage expectations. Without expectations, the entire company seems to just float along rather than striving to achieve goals as a team.

5. You can enjoy your work. Many people agree that they love their job but hate their toxic workplace. There is a huge sense of relief when you can go into work and not have to fear the atmosphere.

How to Form Boundaries at Work

In the first place, you need to understand what your personal boundaries are.

What type of jokes do you find funny, and where is the line that makes them offensive? How much physical contact is enough for you, and similarly, how much of your personal life are you willing to share?

Next, it is time to communicate them. I have included some simple phrases that you can use in a variety of settings, but have the confidence to adapt them to suit your boundary.

If you aren't ready for a short "No," you can use the softer versions. Just never say more than you have to.

———

Your boss wants you to come back to work on a Friday night.

• No, I can't.

• Sorry, I can't, but I'm available tomorrow morning.

• I'd love to help you, but I have plans.

You co-worker has sent you a demanding email – all in capital letters.

• Thank you for considering me, but that's not going to work for me today.

• I wish you'd asked sooner.

• I'll check my schedule for later.

• No, I'm afraid not.

• I understand your urgency, but I'd appreciate it if you didn't email in this way.

Your co-worker keeps insisting you go out with them.

• I don't date colleagues.

• I'm flattered, but no, thank you.

• I'm dedicated to my work.

• I'm not available.

Your manager is manipulating you into giving a presentation you aren't ready for.

• This is John's area, not mine.

• I'd be happy to if I could have a day or two to prepare.

• This isn't in my job description.

• My workload is already full.

A colleague makes discriminatory jokes.

- That isn't funny.

- That type of humor disgusts me.

- If you continue to tell jokes like this, I'll report you.

- Wow, I thought that humor went out with the 80s.

Your colleague has recently been promoted and is on a power trip.

- Congratulations on your promotion, but I still know how to handle my role.

- I feel that you're abusing your power and not respecting my experience.

- You deserve this promotion, but there is no need to treat me like the fool.

A person in your office invades your personal space.

- I feel uncomfortable with personal contact.

- I'm sorry, but I'm not a touchy-feely kind of person.

- Your physical proximity is too much for me.

- Would you mind taking a step back?

The new kid is trying to reinvent the wheel.

- I'm more than happy to listen to your ideas, but at a more appropriate time.

- We're on a tight deadline. Let's focus on the task at hand, and then look at your suggestions.

• Your enthusiasm hasn't gone unnoticed. Perhaps you can draft an email so I can take a closer look.

• I appreciate your recent qualifications, but experience is just as crucial.

A co-worker is disrespecting the janitor.

• I find your behavior unacceptable for a positive working environment like ours.

• There's nothing wrong with earning a decent living.

• Not everyone has had your opportunities.

(It will very much depend on the type of comment, and it doesn't have to be the cleaning crew. The point is, when you see other people being treated unfairly, stand up for them.)

It's always better to address work boundaries as they come up. If you've ever had something on the tip of your tongue and not been able to say it, you'll know how frustrated you feel afterward. This frustration leads to self-tormenting, regret, and wasted time.

Don't force yourself when you aren't ready. With practice, it will become more natural for you to enforce the boundary in the moment.

You can take a couple of minutes to compose your thoughts, or wait until the other person is on their own. But the longer you leave it, the more likely your colleague is to cross the boundary again, and the harder it becomes for you to deal with it.

Make Technology Part of Your Boundaries

It's true that I've complained about the effects of modern technology on communication, but in the workplace, it's an absolutely amazing tool to help with boundaries.

Project management tools are fantastic ways for your colleagues to share tasks and update progress. The team can see exactly what needs to be done and what different people are working on at the time. Individual deadlines and team deadlines can be posted. Delegating becomes easier, as you can see who already has too much to do and who could pull their socks up a little.

With built-in communication tools, you can also keep everyone in the loop. If a meeting has been canceled, everyone gets to find out at the same time instead of someone wasting their time waiting because they didn't receive the memo.

Make sure that your digital tools also have their boundaries. Limit chat to professional comments only, and make sure it's only used within office hours.

Social events at work are very important. They provide us with the opportunity to get to know each other better, and most importantly, to learn about personal boundaries.

That's not to say that the office BBQ should be used as a show and tell for boundaries. It's a chance to relax and enjoy time without the stress of work. Though it is a social event, remain professional at all times, regardless of whether it is your first wheel or you're the CEO. It will be almost impossible for you to assert your boundaries in the office if your colleagues are imagining you doing karaoke after too many drinks.

———

Practice Your Work Boundaries

It's a good idea to first write a list of the areas you would like to see change. Play out conversations where first you play the boundary violator, and then you play yourself.

Even if you feel a little crazy, use a mirror so that you can focus on your body language, and in particular, your facial expressions.

If you have had success setting boundaries with a friend or family member, ask them to role play with you. Even better, if you know someone in the office who is having the same difficulties as you, practice together.

Expressing your boundaries in the workplace may require a different kind of confidence, as you aren't as close to co-workers as you are to your friends. The more practice you can have, whether it's with the mirror, your pet, or another person, the greater your confidence will be.

Finally, take time off. Take every day and every hour you're entitled to. When someone emails you or texts you when you're in yoga or taking your kids to soccer practice, send a quick message back saying, "Let's talk about it on Monday morning," or, "I don't take work calls/texts/emails out of hours."

Remember that as more of us are working remotely

nowadays, it doesn't mean to say we're on call 24/7. It's essential for your own wellbeing that you have a chance to disconnect from both your job and your colleagues.

Nobody can afford to let work stress make them sick. Without this break, you'll remain in the already large percentage of people suffering from work stress.

CHAPTER 11: DEALING WITH DIFFICULT PEOPLE: HOW TO MAINTAIN YOUR BOUNDARIES WHEN SOMEONE VIOLATES THEM

In a perfect world, you will have expressed your boundaries to the people you love, and they will have understood completely, allowing you to lead the life that you imagined. We live in a far from perfect world, and you are going to get pushback, and this is where our final C comes into play – control.

You may have already experienced this painful experience, and are starting to wonder if there's any point in continuing. Our focus has to be on maintaining your boundaries, but even before that, it's about remembering your decision and standing by it.

It's about keeping the image of you in a place where you are free to make your own choices without fear of repercussions. It is this image that's going to help you to cope with the reactions of those who aren't going to accept your boundary easily.

Before looking at how we're going to deal with difficult

people, I think it's important to learn how to stick to our own decisions.

Whether you have made the decision to establish one boundary or 10, keep these small steps in mind:

• Don't wait a long time in between making your decision and executing it. The longer you wait, the more time you have to doubt it.

• Get excited about your decision. Visualizing the results is one way, but you might also want to be a little more creative. Make a board showing some of the things you want to do with the spare time you create, like new hobbies you wish to start or other new goals.

• Wake up every morning and remind yourself about your decision. Think of a powerful mantra like, "Today I will carry out my decisions."

• When you have moments of doubt, pull yourself back to the present and think of the result you're going to achieve.

• Take time to give yourself a pat on the back. There will be more celebratory moments when your boundaries are respected, but for now, don't forget to celebrate the fact that you have made this life changing decision.

• Share your decisions with someone who will not only support you, but also get excited about your decision. These are the people who are going to motivate you to keep going when someone violates your boundary.

When Is It Really a Violation of Boundaries?

Throughout this book, we've looked at a number of

boundary-crossing scenarios that one person would say are okay, and the next would agree that are unacceptable. We began in the initial chapters with the importance of understanding your own boundaries, and the subsequent chapters have been about learning to deal with boundaries related to specific types of relationships. In each type of relationship, there are going to be people who either push your boundary or just completely disregard it.

You will feel like this is your fault, and that you haven't expressed the boundary clearly. Truth be told, you have executed your boundary to perfection, but by definition, there are two sides to a boundary – your limit and the ideals of the other person.

If people are still pushing your boundaries, it's not because you're doing it wrong. It's on them and their beliefs, views and ideals.

You will have to get tougher. Your communication will have to be clearer, and your consequences more extreme. You can't feel bad about this in any way because you are only responsible for your own emotions.

On that note, you need to turn all of your negative emotions, such as fear, worry, guilt and selfishness, into positive energy and strength. Give yourself a stern talking to: "Hang on a minute, I expressed a wish, kindly and respectfully, and the other person has reacted as if I don't exist. That's wrong!"

Remember that this isn't the same as establishing your boundary. We have already considered what needs to be achieved and set boundaries.

Many people won't have been aware of these personal limits you had, and now that they are, they'll respect them. However, violating boundaries is when you have set them, and people continue to disrespect them.

Whether it's unintentional or not, at this point, there should be no excuses, and no letting people off because they didn't realize. Even if it was unintentionally, you have expressed your wishes, and they haven't taken them seriously enough to remember.

A boundary violation is when you have asked someone to stop swearing in front of your children, but they continue to use foul language. You've told your partner repeatedly that you don't like mushrooms, but they add them to every meal. Your boss asks you every weekend to work overtime, even though you've told him that you can't. Perhaps it's your family: Mom and Dad still think it's okay to show up unannounced, or despite being perfectly happy single, your best friend just doesn't stop matchmaking in the most embarrassing way.

It could be any situation where you have clearly stated your discomfort and people continue with the actions that hurt you. Again, name-calling or mocking you might seem relatively small to someone else, but it's having a negative impact on your life, and has to be stopped.

How to Deal With Negative Responses to Boundaries

To put things in perspective and context, we have 10 examples of negative reactions to boundary setting, and examples of what can be said.

#1 But you always help me.

"I have always helped you in the past, but this has taken a toll on me. I'm not saying that I'll never be able to help you, but this time, I'm saying no."

Notice that you have changed 'always help me' to a past action to reinstate that there is a change. For a short answer, use, "That was then. This is now."

#2 I can't believe you're being so selfish.

I was so fed up with someone constantly calling me selfish that I turned around and said, "I can't believe you're being so ironic." I had to explain this to them because they weren't able to see that they were being selfish by not considering my needs.

You can also use phrases like, "I'm not selfish: I'm taking care of myself," or, "Stop calling me selfish. It's unkind and not true."

#3 Ghosting/Silence

When someone gives you the silent treatment, it's because they want a reaction from you, so in this case, you shouldn't say anything.

Take some time to see what life is like without this person in your life. Is it better or worse?

If they're a true friend, they will contact you. If they're a person that you can't simply remove from your life, send a message such as, "Giving me the silent treatment isn't going to make me change my mind. I'm willing to talk to you about it when you're ready."

#4 I hate you.

Take a deep breath, and don't react with anger. These words hurt, but it's unlikely that they mean it. Ask them if that's how they really feel because they will probably say, "No," and you can reply with, "I understand that you don't like what I'm saying, but it's important to me." If they say "Yes," then walk away, at least until they reach out to you with an apology.

#5 If you don't do it, I won't talk to you again.

It's a very immature thing to say, and again, this response is probably lashing out because they don't like you asserting yourself. You may feel the most appropriate response is, "Okay, if that's how you feel." If you don't feel ready to walk away, say something like, "Threatening me isn't going to make me change my mind. If you like, we can look at finding a compromise so we're both happy."

#6 I'll find someone who does want to help me (guilt trip).

Like ghosting, it's a manipulative response, and if you don't stand your ground, it will be that much harder to establish boundaries with this person in the future. They will be expecting you to say that you'll do it.

The best way to reinforce the boundary is to say, "Okay," or, "That's great." You might feel that a phrase like, "It's not that I don't want to help you; it's that I can't," is kinder, but be prepared for the other person to come back with further pushback.

#7 You will never get a promotion if you keep saying no.

This person is trying to scare you into doing things you don't want to do. If they're a colleague, then they have no weight behind the empty threat. If they're a superior, report the issue to human resources.

Your responsibilities and hours are clearly defined in your contract, and they can't not consider you for a promotion for not taking on more than is required of you.

#8 Why do you have to be so cruel to your mom when she's only trying to help you?

Again, we have this word "cruel" that implies you're killing puppies or stealing from old ladies. Your parents still haven't seen that you're only trying to live your life independently. Review the steps for breaking the control cycle.

Phrases you can use could be, "I'm not being cruel. I love all you do for me, and I'm grateful. I'm setting boundaries because I need to focus on my health," or, "I feel very hurt when you call me cruel, and I would appreciate it if you didn't insult me and try to make me feel guilty."

#9 My last partner never complained.

Comparing your partner with a past partner is an absolute boundary violation. You are two completely different people. You have to clearly state that you won't tolerate being compared. "Don't compare me with your ex," "I'm not the same person as your ex," or, "Your ex was entitled to their opinions just like I am," are three examples.

#10 Shouting, insulting. or any sign of physical abuse.

The aim is to calm the person down before reiterating your boundary. If you continue, you run the risk of their temper escalating. Try, "I want to have a conversation with you, and I want to see your point of view, but I can't when you're shouting," or "Let's take a little time to cool down, and then we can talk about it." Don't stay in any situation where you don't feel safe, and I can't stress this enough. It is always better to walk away than to stay and risk being hurt.

How to Protect Your Boundaries

If you're worried about protecting your boundaries, you need to understand that the process is much easier when you're taking care of yourself.

Enforcing boundaries causes stress. The stress is temporary, and each step will get easier, but in those first few weeks and months, take time to do the things you enjoy and to physically experience the benefits of the boundaries you've begun to enforce.

Seeing small improvements is the greatest motivation to protect your boundaries. We'll start with the people who are going to be more open to your boundaries because not everyone is going to push back.

Let's imagine a friend who keeps talking about their sex life, and it's way too much information for you. They're easy to talk to, and the rest of your relationship is great, so you set your boundary by saying, "I love that you have an amazing sex life, but could you please tone down the details?" The problem is solved, and you can reward yourself for a fantastic job. The relief is encouraging, and it will help you to not only protect this boundary, but also the others that you're preparing.

What If Your Boundaries Are Pushed: How to Stand Up for Yourself

Standing up for yourself is very similar to not having boundaries in the first place. There's often a deep-rooted reason for why you can't stand up for yourself. It might be that your parents were overly strict and you didn't have the chance to stand up for yourself, or you've learned over time that your standing up for yourself means putting your needs before others, and society has taught us that this is wrong. The first thing to do is to get to the bottom of this and ask yourself why you don't feel you can stand up for yourself.

Look at all of the situations in which you wish you'd stood up for yourself. Use these as practice scenarios. Imagine what you would have said. Think about "I" statements you could have used:

● I don't appreciate it when…

● I would like it if…

● I feel...when you…

● I'm not prepared to…

● I need...

Initially, you will feel guilty, but that's not to say that you're doing the wrong thing. You need to keep telling yourself that guilt is just an emotion that has no place in this process.

If people don't respect you for standing up for yourself, it's time to decide whether they're toxic people in your life and if the relationship is worth saving. The toxic people in your life may need special treatment. Here are a few more specific tips.

How to Deal With Difficult People

- Be empathetic, and try to understand where they're coming from.

- Actively listen to what they're saying.

- Don't engage with people who yell or shout.

- Highlight someone's inappropriate behavior, such as the silent treatment or passive aggression.

- Decide if you want this person in your life.

A co-worker invited you out on a date and you kindly declined. They have now started spreading rumors about you to overcome their rejection. You can see that their ego has been damaged, but also understand that their behavior is both passive-aggressive (playing the victim) and socially aggressive.

You can take the person to one side and say, "I'm sorry that you were hurt by my no, but that's no excuse to speak badly of me. I'd like to find a way for us to work together in a friendly way. If your behavior continues, I'll have no option but to talk to human resources."

How to Deal With Manipulators

● Ignore all manipulative behavior. Don't fall into their trap.

● Don't feel the urge to fit in with them.

● Trust yourself and your judgment.

● Resist compromising.

● Decide if you want this person in your life.

You tell your aunt that you can't make Christmas dinner. She starts with some overly dramatic statements that play on your emotions – your parents are going to be devastated, it's the first family Christmas in years, and who knows if dear old Granny will be around for the next one, or something along those lines. You need to tell your aunt, "My parents are my problem. It might be the first family Christmas in years, but we're together every month, and dear old Granny's only concerned that her family is happy." This is the end of the conversation, so change the subject.

How to Deal With a Narcissist

● Remember that narcissists rarely change.

● Remember that a narcissist will go to any length to make you look bad.

● Don't play their behavior down.

● Don't try to compete with a narcissist.

● Decide whether you want this person in your life.

You cook dinner for friends, and the narcissist finds every reason to complain and belittle your efforts. "Oh, paper napkins — classy!"

They constantly watch your reactions, waiting for a reaction, each comment becoming harsher and more obvious than the next.

Every snarky comment has to wash over you as if it was no more than a raindrop. Take control of the conversation with your other guests, and bring up positive, entertaining topics so that the narcissist can't ruin the evening.

If it becomes too much or your guests are becoming uncomfortable, keep a smile on your face, and say, "If you aren't enjoying the evening, you're more than welcome to leave."

How to Deal With a Toxic Person

• Speak up and let them know that you don't accept their toxicity.

• Don't take their behavior to heart.

• Be compassionate but don't excuse.

• Be careful of toxic mood swings where people run hot and cold – this shouldn't be tolerated either.

• Decide if you want this person in your life.

You're talking to a group of friends about the *Black Lives Matter* movement. Your friend interrupts you and says, "They're all being dramatic and need to find something better to do with their lives," and they know this attitude will hurt you.

You can say, "Everyone's entitled to their opinion, but I find yours insensitive and offensive. This is now a topic I won't discuss with you." If they continue, say, "No." Stand up, and walk away. Toxic people will often cross hard boundaries related to your ethics, and you need to be true to yourself.

How to Deal With Emotional Drainers

- Limit your contact with them, especially when you're exhausted.

- Explain that you're there for them, but that you also need to take care of yourself.

- Teach them about boundaries.

- Find ways to recharge your batteries.

- Decide if you want this person in your life.

Your friend complains about everything – the weather, their partner, their job, the last thing they watched on TV – and nothing makes them happy. Every time you meet them, you come away feeling depressed and deflated.

Here's a great quote to get them thinking: "The grass isn't greener on the other side. The grass is greener where you water it."

You have to teach this person that you too have problems, and sometimes you want to talk about them. You also need to explain that complaining only gets them so far in life; they have the ability to change their own situation.

Stop answering every phone call and every text. Say, "I'm here for you, but I need some time to myself to recharge."

How to Deal With a People Pleaser

- Empathize with them.

- Ask for their opinions and ideas.

- Encourage them to make decisions about what you do together.

- Encourage them to get professional help.

- Decide if you want this person in your life.

It might sound ironic because more often than not, we are the people pleasers. However, it's still difficult to establish boundaries with someone who says yes to everything.

Imagine you're planning a party for your parents, and your sibling says yes to every idea. Having their input would make the party so much better. "I know you're happy with anything, but I would appreciate your ideas."

Instead of asking yes/no questions, ask questions that require an opinion. Replace, "Does Mom like purple flowers?" with "What color flowers does Mom like?" Praise them for making choices.

You will notice that with each type of person, you need to decide if you want them in your life. It's a decision only you can make, and it will be a hard one, but ask your compass, and have faith in it. You aren't mean, cruel or selfish; you're making an essential decision that will improve the quality of your life.

Boundary-Setting Troubleshooting

Finally, we will look at real life situations that people have struggled to overcome.

Troubleshooting #1: My family is an enmeshed family unit. None of us have boundaries, and any time I try to express mine, people call me selfish and say that I only think of myself.

Solution: Enmeshment is a complex family dysfunction. First of all, decide if there is another family member who is inclined to agree with you. It will be easy to have an open family conversation with someone who shares your feelings.

Create a safe environment for the conversation at a time that is suitable for everyone; make sure there's no rush. Speak openly about how you feel and the changes that you want to make: "I understand that this is something you don't agree with, but I need to make some changes so that I can feel happier in our family. I love you all, and this is the main reason for my decision."

Listen to how your family feels, and if they insult you, say, "This is exactly my point. I feel hurt when you call me selfish, but you don't appear to care about my feelings." Always keep the conversation on track, but stay calm.

Troubleshooting #2: I hate feeling like a nag all the time. I've tried explaining the problem, but it doesn't sink in.

Solution: Consequences. I had a friend whose partner went out, and at least once a month, would come home drunk at 6 am. There were no trust issues, but he was drinking and driving at nearly 40, and with a baby on the way. He didn't understand that this behavior was unacceptable. She had so many conversations and arguments, and even took his keys away, but it didn't make a difference.

One day he said, "You're such a typical woman: always nagging." She said, "I'm not going to nag anymore. If you aren't home by 3 am, you're locked out until 6 pm the next day because you aren't treating our home like a hotel."

And the next time, he was locked out until 6 pm the next day. He came home, and there was no fight because everything was clear. Stop nagging, set your consequences, and follow through with them.

Troubleshooting #3: I've been direct about it, and even explained why it bothers me, but it hasn't made any difference.

Solution: The problem here is that although you feel you've been direct, you may not be using the right words to express your feelings and how much you're suffering.

Try having another conversation, but use more powerful adjectives. Instead of bother, use hurt, pain, anger and frustration. Remind the person that you've been patient and already tried to have this conversation.

Tell them that it's not right that you have to put up with

such behavior. Find a consequence that is appropriate, and stick to it.

Troubleshooting #4: My family gets mad at me when I set a boundary. They shout and yell, and I always end up in tears.

Solution: On the one hand, your family may be looking at you as an emotional wreck who's not mature enough to set their own boundaries and live independently. If this is the case, to the first thing you need to do is work on some techniques to recognize your feelings and then learn to control them.

Try keeping a journal to work through your emotions. When you become better at controlling your emotions, you'll be more prepared to handle their anger. "I want to talk to you, but I'm not going to get involved in a fight, and I won't stay if you start getting mad."

As you have set the consequence, you need to follow through. As soon as someone raises their voice, leave. It may take a few attempts, but your family will learn that they're going to have to control their tempers if they want a relationship with you.

Troubleshooting #5: I'm an adult but still living at home. My family are toxic people who won't respect or even listen to my boundaries.

Solution: If you've tried all of the techniques we've worked on so far and nothing has worked, the safest thing for you to do is to create distance.

Find a hobby that takes you out of the house. Exercise will

help you to start feeling better about yourself and provide you with more energy.

Make your room your safe place so that you're happy to spend more time there. Get excited about financial goals so that you can save up for your own place. If things get really bad, stay with a friend or another family member.

Troubleshooting #6: My partner is toxic. I feel like if I end the relationship, I'm the failure, but I'm not sure what else I can do.

Solution: Ending a toxic relationship is not a sign of failure: it's a sign of strength. It's not an easy decision to make, but take a close look and see if the negatives outweigh the positives. Is your physical or mental health suffering?

If you still feel there's hope, try writing down your feelings. Sometimes, when we have the chance to read them out, we don't get angry or start to shout. You have time to gather your thoughts and speak the truth without the fear of a reaction. You don't get interrupted, and the other person can re-read what you have to say as many times as necessary.

Troubleshooting #7: I'm fed up with feeling like I don't have the right to say no, or that I need to explain why I'm saying it.

Solution: You're halfway there already. You have recognized that you shouldn't have to explain every decision you make. Take this feeling of frustration, and use it as energy and confidence.

Try saying, "Because I said no," "No, is my final answer," "You don't have the right to ask me," or, "It's private." Then change the subject. If people continue to question your no, walk away.

Troubleshooting #8: I can't shake the feeling of guilt because I ended an unhealthy friendship. I feel bad because they might need me, or I worry that I could have done more.

Solution: It's perfectly normal to feel guilty, but instead of trying to bury this guilt, accept it and put it to one side. Try to remember that, sadly, they don't need you, and they've probably moved on to the next person.

Know in your heart that you made the right decision and that you will continue to take the same approach. Don't let your past experience with friendships make you fear creating new ones.

Troubleshooting #9: I don't know how many times I should keep trying to establish my boundaries.

Solution: There's no magic number: it will depend on the importance of your relationship with the person. For general acquaintances and colleagues, I have a three-strike rule before creating distance from them, but the number is a personal choice.

Rather than a number, think of your emotional limit. At what point do you feel that you can't take any more? Stop before you reach this limit so you know that you're protecting yourself.

Troubleshooting #10: I feel like my superiors at work are unprofessional and don't respect boundaries. I don't want to come across as boring, but I feel extremely uncomfortable.

Solution: Document everything. Not in an emotional or snitching way, but stick to the facts. Don't go back on your boundaries or feel that you need to compromise. Reinforce them every time, but when you feel like you're close to your emotional limit, take your concerns to human resources.

If you have a co-worker who shares your concerns, it will help if they could do the same. However, be proactive, and don't just complain about the situation together.

———

Every boundary you establish will require your determination to follow it through, but not until you have driven yourself into an unhealthy place.

Your boundaries will only survive if you know your own limits and when to say no to toxic people and toxic relationships. There's still a hurdle to overcome, and that's letting go of this toxicity that others have created so you can go forward on your road to recovery.

CHAPTER 12: EMOTIONAL DETOX: HOW TO RELEASE TOXICITY AND RECOVER FROM A BOUNDARIES CONFLICT

I've met with so many people who have set their boundaries and worked incredibly hard to maintain them within their relationships, and there's always a moment of limbo.

There's a time in between establishing a boundary and the moment when the other person, or people, actually accept it. You may feel like you're walking on eggshells, waiting for the person to explode or revert back to old ways. The people in your life might treat you differently as they are not used to seeing you stand up for yourself and then stick to your decision.

There are other emotionally draining situations during the boundary-setting process. You may have taken some time away from the strain of life to focus on yourself, build up your energy, and learn more about yourself and the boundaries you want to set.

Stepping back into the real world can highlight just how

desperately boundaries are needed, and you might have to adjust your expectations, adding more boundaries to your list than you had first thought necessary.

Of course, if you have had to end relationships, there's still going to be a huge amount of pain that has to be dealt with before you can hope to create new, meaningful relationships.

We've looked at how to build up our energy before expressing boundaries. Practicing emotional control during difficult situations will help you to manage boundary conflict. Now we're going to look at how beneficial an emotional detox is in order to move on with your life in the most positive way.

How to Stay Calm and Control Emotions in Boundary Conflict

There will always be times in our lives when we experience conflict, before, during and after enforcing our boundaries. This isn't necessarily a bad thing. It's good to feel passionate about things, and others are allowed to feel the same passion.

However, how we handle this conflict speaks to our emotional intelligence, our ability to recognize and manage our emotions, and our ability to recognize the emotions of others while appreciating that we can only control our own feelings.

This is a life skill that will help you in so many different situations.

1. Take a few deep breaths and concentrate on what your body is telling you.

Deep breaths prevent us from reacting to the other person's emotions. We have all been in situations when someone snaps as we snap back. Controlled, deep breaths help to reduce the stress hormones, adrenaline and cortisol. This is also an essential few seconds when you can focus on the parts of your body that become tense, and relax those areas.

2. Listen with both ears.

A boundary isn't just expressing what you want. It's about strengthening a relationship. To do this, you need to listen to the other person's point of view. Not listening may irritate the person you're talking to and increase the tension. It's not until they've said all that they have to say that you'll have all of the information to continue the conversation.

3. Stick to questions that require more than a yes or no answer.

Most yes and no answers don't give you more information. More often than not, we tend to ask questions that we want to hear the answer to. Questions that begin with why, what, how, etc. will encourage dialogue.

4. Don't shout.

Don't raise your voice. When we raise our voices, our tone changes. A change in tone and an increase in volume can appear like aggressive behavior, and the other person is likely to retaliate with more conflict. Calming your voice will encourage the other person to mimic your behavior.

5. Appreciate that there are times you won't agree.

You won't agree with everyone all the time, and they won't always agree with you. While it's great to see a point of view and accept it, sometimes you just have to say, "Okay, I love where you're coming from, but I don't agree. Let's agree to disagree." Both parties have expressed their opinions, and the conversation has ended before things get heated.

Quick Tips for Dealing With Confrontation

● Act as soon as you feel emotionally and mentally prepared. The longer you wait, the bigger the issue becomes.

● Give yourself time to feel your emotions before acting.

● Try to deal with the issue in person, and in a neutral environment.

● Choose a time when neither of you is in a hurry or stressed about another issue.

● Keep your goals in mind so that you can focus on the change and not the person.

● Smile, but make sure it's a genuine smile. A smile shows others that you aren't looking for an argument, and that you're positively looking for a solution.

Putting It into practice

If you feel that the boundary you're about to establish is likely to cause a conflict, practice beforehand. Begin with a few minutes of calm breathing to centralize your thoughts. Imagine your conversation going well, the phrases you use, and the reactions of the other person. Play out different reactions and your response to each one. Get comfortable role-playing how you handle conflict.

The best preparation is to imagine the worst-case scenario, and practice how you will handle this. This isn't about assuming the worst or thinking negatively. It's about having every angle covered so you feel more confident in handling conflict, whether it is just a little bit of grumpiness or full-blown rage.

The All-Important Emotional Detox After Conflict and/or Emotional or Physical Abuse

Barbara Ford Shabazz, a clinical psychologist at South University in Savannah, Georgia, has described an emotional detox as the activities and behaviors that allow us to remove any emotions that negatively impact our mental health and physical health. The seven steps below will help you to carry out your emotional detox.

1. Emotional detoxing requires honesty

There's a strong link between our bodies, hearts and minds. There are good connections, and there are negative connections. It's the negative emotions that are connecting to our bodies that we need to understand: this will enable us to find the paths we need to clear.

2. Create a step-by-step plan

A plan of what you want to achieve will keep you focused on specific goals, both in the short term and the long term. Include the triggers that cause stress, hurt, rage, etc.

3. Take a break from social media

Scrolling through people's feeds leaves you wide open to posts that can greatly affect your mood. Furthermore, it's easy to start comparing your life with the lives of others based on photos that often don't reflect the truth.

4. Know your vices

Some people turn to food; others turn to alcohol or drugs, and some people exercise as a way of combating stress. Before heading for your go-to stress vice, take a moment for self-reflection.

5. Learn how to forgive yourself

We make mistakes, and this is normal. Mistakes are how we learn. Take the lesson with you to become a better person, but forgive yourself and move on.

6. Mentally declutter

A full mind is exhausting, and it can prevent us from getting a good night's sleep, concentrating on our work, and engaging in meaningful relationships. Use your journal to take everything that is on your mind and feel the weight lifting off you.

7. Take time to enjoy the good

Gradually, as the pain starts to fade, there will be space in your life and emotions. As you start to recover, you will be able to experience positive experiences: a moment of uncontrollable laughter, the excitement of meeting new people, etc. Relish these positive emotions.

Controlling your emotions and an emotional detox isn't about not feeling. We need negative emotions to help us survive. They are the keys to identifying other health issues.

———

This chapter has taught you the importance of accepting your negative emotions, taking time to process them, using them to your advantage and then letting them go. It will take practice and perseverance. It's all about the temporary stress of boundary-setting that clears the way for the next stage.

CHAPTER 13: LIFE AFTER BOUNDARIES: HOW TO KEEP LOVE IN YOUR RELATIONSHIPS WITH PEOPLE

Not everything in your future is going to be focused on boundaries. It will become a natural part of who you are. You will start to find it easier to express your boundaries without feeling awkward, or as if you're demanding too much from others. You will notice this when you feel the need to readdress your boundaries and adapt them for different stages of your life.

In this final chapter, we're going to look at life after creating boundaries. We'll focus on making sure we don't go from one extreme to the other, and being the best person we can possibly be in order to take our existing and new relationships to a whole new level.

Balance Our Boundaries

If you've been badly hurt in the past, you might find that you go a little over the top with your boundaries. You won't be alone because it's a form of self-protection, and many of us do it.

Imagine a woman who has had several bad relationships because she falls in love far too quickly and then gets called easy. Her new boundary is to date without any form of physical contact until after at least 4 weeks.

What happens here is that she meets a perfect man, but because of her extreme boundary, the dates don't move on as they would have naturally. He feels that she isn't attracted to him, and the relationship is over before it even begins.

She would have done well to explain her boundary to her date, but she was unsure of how to do it without making it all about her ex.

I've seen cases where friends are too scared to ask a person for help because they're worried about crossing a person's new boundary. So, while they have established the boundary well, the communication still needs to be improved so that the friends can appreciate the balance.

Relationships will improve, and you'll both be able to get to know each other on a deeper level, and this is a great moment as you work together to discover your middle ground and to respect the new boundaries, but also to appreciate the freedom that comes with it, the new sense of love, regardless of what type of relationship it is.

Knowing When to Say Yes

If you're having trouble reading your compass for a yes or no answer, there are some other questions to ask yourself before making a decision.

If you are put on the spot, never feel pressured into making a choice straight away because nine times out of 10, you will give the answer others want to hear. Remember: if you aren't sure, ask for more time. During this time, ask yourself the following questions:

- What will you need to sacrifice if you say yes – your free time, or a plan with someone else?

- Find out if the question needs an answer straight away. If you're offered a promotion, will the offer still be there next month?

- Does your yes come with any risks?

- Are there any hidden motives behind the question?

- If the shoe was on the other foot, would this person do the same for you?

With the answers to these questions, you'll be able to decide if you really do want to say yes, and if it's for the right reasons. Learning how to say no is crucial, but don't make it your only answer. It's great that you've mastered how to put your own needs first, but in a successful relationship, it's about both people's needs having equal importance.

Two-Way Boundaries to Keep Relationships Healthy

Now that your relationships are starting to settle and you can see the benefits of your boundaries, it's worth taking a moment to look at things from another perspective: the boundaries of other people. Helping others to express and maintain their boundaries is an excellent way to emphasize a safe environment for both of you.

- Make sure you're giving the other person enough

personal space. It's great that you've identified when you need time alone, but don't let your loved one focus so much on your wellbeing that they forget to take care of themselves.

- Get excited about their interests and achievements. Showing someone you care about the things that excite them allows them to feel like you genuinely care about them. It's not the right time to tell them about your exciting news, as it will take away their special moment.

- Ask permission before borrowing things. Until a person tells you that you don't have to ask, it's respectful to ask first. Siblings have a habit of taking things, and this can stick with them into adulthood, but it's not okay. You should also ask permission before entering personal space, even if it's just a knock on the door.

- Don't criticize the people you care about. Body shaming is a massive problem that both men and women suffer from. If someone asks you for advice, choose your words and your tone carefully so that it doesn't come across as offensive.

- This stage might seem like you've rebooted your relationship and it's similar to those first moments. You're more tempted to send messages and call, but make sure you aren't overdoing it.

- Checking someone's phone is the equivalent of reading their journal. Aside from showing that you don't trust them, you also risk breaching privacy and confidentiality if they use their phone for work.

- Always check with people before you post images of them on social media. Not everybody has the same boundaries when it comes to their personal life online. In the case of social media, asking before posting can prevent conflict.

- Protect your independence. As you start to become closer again, check that this closeness doesn't convert into dependency. If you feel like you can't make decisions without them or you don't want to do things alone, take a step back, and reassess your emotions.

- Don't be a snooper! By paying close attention to what people are saying, you can get an idea of what they're comfortable talking about and what they aren't. It's natural to want to ask questions to start a conversation or learn more, but try to keep them general. Asking someone about when they're going to settle down or start a family looks like prying rather than caring.

- Keep every promise you make. Breaking promises leads to distrust and a feeling that you don't care. If you aren't sure you can do something, don't promise it.

- Never go to bed on an argument, even if it isn't with your partner. First of all, the chances are, you won't sleep well. Secondly, the issue won't just disappear: it will fester.

Recreating Love for All of Your Relationships

If you've had to take some space away from people you love, the first few interactions might be straining or tense. It won't be like this forever. After a few visits, you'll both start to relax and feel more confident with your interactions.

Don't bring up the past. It has been dealt with, and it is

now time to move forward. If the other person brings it up, you can choose to listen if they feel that they need to communicate their feelings.

If you feel like the conversation isn't productive, don't interrupt, but just say, "I think we discussed our problems in the past, and now I would love to focus on getting things back on track for the future." In the first few interactions, keep the conversation quite light and positive.

It's really important at this stage that you listen and read their boundary signs, while making sure that yours are protected. Keep visits and activities short so that nobody outstays their welcome. Gradually, you can plan activities that last longer.

It's the comfort and security that you both feel while being able to communicate openly that will lead to having fun together, and when you're having fun, love is soon to follow.

———

Put It into Practice

Think about the following questions and how you would answer them:

- Your best friend wants you to be their bridesmaid/best man – yes or no?

- Your kid wants to borrow your car but never fills up the tank – yes or no?

- You want to meet your parents after a few months of

little to no contact. Will you agree to lunch at their house or coffee in a neutral location?

- Your sibling has posted photos of you on Facebook. How will you react?

- What would you say to the colleague who got promoted before you?

- Your partner doesn't feel that your boundaries are fair or balanced. How will you work on compromises?

TYING IT ALL TOGETHER

R eaching the end of a book like this is just the beginning. There has been plenty of information, techniques, tips, and things to start practicing. Some people feel motivated, others overwhelmed by what might lie ahead.

While you should feel prepared to begin, remember that the first step is reflection. It's likely that you have been through some extremely stressful, and possibly traumatic, experiences.

Don't rush into making any changes before you've taken some time for self-care and to gain your strength. This is the key to getting the next stages right.

You don't need to be fit for a marathon or feel that you have all the confidence in the world. But you do need to be in the right place, both physically and emotionally.

To summarize all of the information, we can look at the 3

Cs — create your boundaries, communicate your boundaries, and then control them.

To create your boundaries, look hard at yourself and your life to decide where you need to see changes and when you want them. The changes that you need are your first priority because they're things that are affecting your wellbeing. The things that you want are the smaller boundaries that will allow you to enjoy your life to the fullest.

Write a list of your boundaries, and be clear on those that are an absolute no, and those that you would be willing to compromise on. The planning stage is so important because it will help you to feel prepared before communicating your boundaries.

When you're confident, your loved ones will see that you're calm, collected, and above all, serious. Prepare some short sentences, keeping the focus on your feelings rather than the person's behavior. This is where the "I" statements will help. Have backup phrases in case there's some push back from the other person.

You will know when you're ready to communicate your boundaries. It could be at the time of a boundary violation. If you don't feel like the circumstances are right, wait for the time that is.

You should try to keep the time between the boundary violation and the communication as short as possible, but if the room is full of people or if emotions are too high, ask to speak to the person a little later. Take a few minutes for deep breathing, meditation, or even just watch your favorite

YouTube video – whatever helps you to get into the right mindset.

Don't push your emotions down: take this time to feel them and understand their roots, and then leave them to one side. Keep your head high and your shoulders back, make eye contact, and keep your tone at the appropriate level.

Once you have communicated your boundary, bear in mind that you have done the right thing in the right way. It's now up to them to control their emotions. Stand by your decision, no matter what. Don't let people try to manipulate you or make you feel like you don't have the right to express your boundary. At any point that you don't feel comfortable, walk away.

It will be easier to control your boundaries with some people than it will with others. Mom might not accept your boundary straight away because she could think you're being dramatic.

Toxic people may insult, threaten, manipulate or scare you. You neither deserve this, nor have to put up with it. You have every right to put your needs first. Ending a toxic relationship can be harder, and it is a personal decision.

Professional help is nothing to be ashamed of. Sometimes, our traumas are so deeply rooted within us that it takes a professional to help us untangle them. And, please, remember that your safety must come first.

The stress caused by creating boundaries has to be controlled. You might want to dance, scream, do yoga, talk to a friend, or curl up with a book.

Notice your emotional triggers, and when stress becomes too much, go to your stress releasing place. This stress will not last forever.

Soon, you will be able to see the amazing impact of your boundary setting, even if it's just small steps. Celebrate every win, take each day one at a time, and remain determined to achieve the wonderful life you have envisioned.

SOME BOOKS YOU MAY FIND INTERESTING

Stop People Pleasing

How to Start Saying No, Set Healthy Boundaries, and Express Yourself

Do you say yes to people so often, you've forgotten how it feels to say no?

You're not alone.

Many people spend years putting aside their own wants and needs in order to please the people in their life and avoid conflict. Although there will always be situations where diplomacy is important, **you cannot define your life through other people**.

There's a fine line between being considerate of others, and compromising your individuality, and you can slip into living as a people-pleaser without even realizing it.

Maybe you've been going through the routines of life feeling that you must keep quiet, and take responsibility for the feelings of others.

Or, maybe you think it's more important to avoid "rocking the boat" than it is to be **your most authentic self**.

While these habits might seem to dominate everything you do, there are actionable steps you can take to create a new world--one where you are open and confident in what you say and do.

Just like the relationships you have with others, everyone's experiences with people-pleasing are unique. However, this individuality often stems from common roots that are keeping you trapped in the box of others' expectations.

By helping you identify the steps that will assist you the most, Chase Hill shows it is possible to start changing, right here and right now.

In *Stop People Pleasing*, you will discover:

• The **10 signs** that indicate people-pleasing characteristics, besides the inability to say no

• A step-by-step **14-day action plan** to help you achieve instant and notable improvements

• The **4 defense mechanisms specific to people pleasing**, how to identify them, and how to respond to them

• Multiple exercises and approaches to help you rediscover who you are at heart, breaking free from feeling the need to seek validation from others

• Coping mechanisms designed to help you overcome discomfort or frustration as you redefine the boundaries in your life

And much more.

If you believe it's impossible to finally stand up to your in-laws or be honest with your friends, think again.

You deserve to **make the choices that YOU want to make**, and speak your mind without fear or anxiety.

There's no quick fix for people-pleasing. Like most important things, changing your patterns will take time.

With the right tools and techniques by your side, you will be able to hit the ground running and be one step closer to living your life the way *you* want to live it.

If you're ready to finally stand up for yourself and transform your life, scan the QR code below to order this book from Amazon page!

How to Stop Overthinking

The 7-Step Plan to Control and Eliminate Negative Thoughts, Declutter Your Mind and Start Thinking Positively in 5 Minutes or Less

Do you find yourself lying awake at night because you can't stop worrying about what happened today? Are you constantly second-guessing almost every decision that you are faced with in life? Do your job, friendships or whole life seem to be overwhelming?

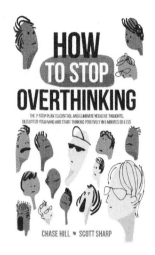

By reading this book, you will emboldened yourself to deal with your fears, anxiety, handle your perfectionism, and stop your overthinking for good.

What you should expect along the journey of practicing the techniques and strategies throughout this book is to be aware of where your mental chatter comes from, and how to address it.

Stop worrying about what you did today and start living in the moment. Stop living for tomorrow and start breathing in the positivity of today. Stop overthinking your future and make big changes to live your future now.

We are only ever promised today, so instead of obsessing over what you could have done at that social event or trying to control what you will do in your next appointment, learn to breathe in this moment you have now.

What you'll learn:

• How to Control Overthinking and Eliminate Negative Thoughts in Just a Few Minutes.

- 10 Powerful Tactics to Stop Anxiety and Worrying Permanently.

- How to Sleep Better, Even if Your Head Is Full of Thoughts.

- Simple Tips to Develop Self-Confidence and Decision-Making Skills.

- How to Remove Toxicity and Change Your Relationships for the Better.

- 5 Ways to Calm Anxiety (Worrying) in Five Minutes or Less.

- Troubleshooting Guide if Nothing Helps.

- How to Declutter Your Mind and Become What You Want in Life.

This book will go through the reasons why the way you think now is not beneficial to your being and how positivity can greatly improve your outlook and put yourself in the direction you want your life to go.

So, quit being stuck, stop letting your mind trap you, and take control of what you want. There are finally lessons and a structure to get you to where you **want** to be rather than where you are now. AND, it's all in this book.

Would You Like To Know More?

Grab this book to get started and turn off your overthinking for good!

Scan the QR code below to order it from Amazon immediately.

Assertiveness Training

How to Stand Up for Yourself, Boost Your Confidence, and Improve Assertive Communication Skills

Stop being a pushover – it's time for you to be seen, be heard, and to get what you deserve.

Have you spent the better portion of your life physically and mentally unable to strive for what you **really want**, passively riding the waves as they come?

Are you constantly considerate of others' feelings, having made too many compromises in the

CHASE HILL

ASSERTIVENESS TRAINING

HOW TO STAND UP FOR YOURSELF, BOOST YOUR CONFIDENCE, AND IMPROVE ASSERTIVE COMMUNICATION SKILLS

past that have left you feeling unfulfilled and empty?

Do you feel as if you have been walking in unfitted shoes for as long as you can remember, never daring to ask yourself the **most valuable and fundamental** question:

"What do I want for myself?"

You may currently be facing an unsettling internal conflict, wondering how you can assert yourself and express your **genuine** thoughts, needs, and opinions without being aggressive or disliked by those around you.

Your generosity and kindness are indeed a double-edged sword – they may feel like your weaknesses, but you need to realize that they are also two of your most admirable strengths.

Only then will you be able to find real **balance** in your life.

Being assertive isn't synonymous with being aggressive or unfriendly – it is very much possible to be confident and firm all while being **polite and kind**.

True assertiveness, rooted in a real inner **desire to build relationships instead of destroying them**, is a rare and precious commodity among people nowadays.

The mere fact that you're striving for it shows off your undeniable strength and ability to transform and evolve as a human being.

There's no reason to be held back by discomfort and fear anymore – with the right training, your timid nature will undoubtedly subside, making room for the assertive person you've always longed to be.

In *Assertiveness Training*, you will discover:

• How to recognize the **subtle behaviors** that have been hindering your path to self-fulfillment, as well as ways to start transforming them into more positive and self-affirming habits

• **Scientifically proven** steps to practice self-awareness and emotional control to avoid the most common emotional setbacks barricading the way between you and your assertive self

• How to tackle the anxiety and fear that come from your first attempts at being assertive, **making assertiveness second nature**

• A plethora of situation-based tips and tricks that will guide you through the process of knowing exactly what to say and do to let people know that you're not to be walked over

• **Comprehensive guidance** on how to be assertive in your workplace to finally get the recognition and respect you deserve

• How to find the right balance between passive and aggressive behavior to gain genuine respect from others, untainted by pity or fear

• A step-by-step **action plan**, taking you on a transformative journey towards building more confidence that's rooted in a polite and kind contact with the people around you

And much more.

Assertiveness is not a natural-born trait, but it is a skill that we all can acquire with perseverance and the right kind of guidance.

If you want to gain the respect and admiration of others for being who you truly are, scan the QR code below to order this book from Amazon page!

A FREE GIFT TO OUR READERS

I'd like to give you a gift as a way of saying thanks for your purchase!

This checklist includes:

- 8 steps to start saying no.
- 12 must-dos to stop feeling guilty.
- 9 healthy ways to say no.

The last thing we want is for your mood to be ruined because you weren't prepared.

To receive your Say No Checklist, visit the link:

www.chaschillbooks.com

If you have any difficulty downloading the checklist,

contact me at chase@chasehillbooks.com, and I'll send you a copy as soon as possible.

RESOURCES

3 Tactics of Controlling Parents . . . and Ways to Handle and Heal. (2020, January 1). [Video]. YouTube. https://www.youtube.com/watch?v=I8Nd2pCP4UQ

10 Ways to Deal with a Toxic Sibling – Psych2Go. (2017, October 29). Psych2Go. https://psych2go.net/10-ways-to-deal-with-a-toxic-sibling/

A. (2020, August 5). 7 Boundary Exercises for Empaths and Sensitive People. Kind Earth. https://www.kindearth.net/7-boundary-exercises-for-empaths-and-other-sensitive-people/

Abrams, A. (2017, October 1). Overcoming the Need to Please. Psychology Today. https://www.psychologytoday.com/us/blog/nurturing-self-compassion/201710/overcoming-the-need-please

Anderson, M. (2020, October 14). Setting Strong Boundaries When You're Codependent. Love Over Addiction. https://loveoveraddiction.com/boundaries-for-codependents/

Atanacio, A. (2016, February 8). *11 Ways to Handle Confrontation. SUCCESS.* https://www.success.com/11-ways-to-handle-confrontation/

Boundary Setting and Healthy Communication | The Georgia Way. (n.d.). *Thegeorgiaway.* https://thegeorgiaway.com/project/boundary-setting-and-healthy-communication/

Business News Daily Editor. (2020, May 6). *50-Hour Workweeks? How to Cut Back on the New Normal. Business News Daily.* https://www.businessnewsdaily.com/8357-longer-work-weeks.html

Carver, C. (2019, December 26). *Quotes About Boundaries to Help You Set and Honor Them. Be More with Less.* https://bemorewithless.com/quotes-about-boundaries/

Chui, A. (2019, February 28). *The Desire to Be Liked Will End You up Feeling More Rejected. Lifehack.* https://www.lifehack.org/634716/the-desire-to-be-liked-will-end-you-up-feeling-more-rejected

Clarke, J. (2020, July 27). *How to Recognize Someone With Covert Narcissism. Verywell Mind.* https://www.verywellmind.com/understanding-the-covert-narcissist-4584587

Cole, T. (2021). *Boundary Boss.* T. Cole.

Contessa, C. (2021, January 5). *How to Establish Healthy Boundaries at Work. Career Contessa.* https://www.careercontessa.com/advice/healthy-boundaries-at-work/

Earnshaw, E., LMFT. (2019, July 21). *6 Types Of Boundaries You Deserve To Have (And How To Maintain Them). Mindbodygreen.* https://www.mindbodygreen.com/articles/six-types-of-boundaries-and-what-healthy-boundaries-look-like-for-each

Gaba, S. (2019, August 4). *Boundaries and the Dance of the Codependent. Psychology Today.* https://www.psychologytoday.com/us/blog/addiction-and-recovery/201908/boundaries-and-the-dance-the-codependent

Glass, L. J. (2020, November 29). *Codependents & Boundaries: Why Do They Struggle? PIVOT.* https://www.lovetopivot.com/what-cause-triggers-codependency-boundaries-recovery-coaching/

Good boundaries free you | Sarri Gilman | TEDxSnoIsleLibraries. (2015, December 17). *[Video]. YouTube.* https://www.youtube.com/watch?v=rtsHUeKnkC8

Haynes, T. (2021, February 4). *Dopamine, Smartphones & You: A battle for your time. Science in the News.* https://sitn.hms.harvard.edu/flash/2018/dopamine-smartphones-battle-time/

Heckman, W. (2019, September 25). *42 Worrying Workplace Stress Statistics. The American Institute of Stress.* https://www.stress.org/42-worrying-workplace-stress-statistics

Hoskin, M. N. (2021, March 23). *What's an Emotional Detox and Do You Need One? The Healthy.* https://www.thehealthy.com/mental-health/emotional-detox/

J. (2018b, June 18). *What Does Your Tone of Voice Convey? Exploring Your Mind.* https://exploringyourmind.com/what-does-your-tone-of-voice-convey/

Jodi Schulz, Michigan State University Extension. (2021, March 9). *Eye contact: Don't make these mistakes. MSU Extension.* https://www.canr.msu.edu/news/eye_contact_dont_make_these_mistakes

Katherine, A. (2000). *Where to Draw The Line. Fireside.*

Kaufman, S. B. (2011, March 25). DO Narcissists Know They Are Narcissists? Psychology Today. https://www.psychologytoday.com/us/blog/beautiful-minds/201103/do-narcissists-know-they-are-narcissists

King, P. (n.d.). How to Establish Boundaries. P. King.

Lancer, D. (n.d.). Dilemas of Codependent Men. Whatiscodepencency.Com. https://www.whatiscodependency.com/dilemmas-of-codependent-men/

Lancer, D. L. (2020, April 11). Dilemmas of Codependent Men. What Is Codependency? https://www.whatiscodependency.com/dilemmas-of-codependent-men/

Levin, N. (2020, January 17). How Your Fears Prevent You from Setting Boundaries. Nancy Levin. https://nancylevin.com/how-your-fears-prevent-you-from-setting-boundaries/

Li, P. (2021, April 22). 4 Types of Parenting Styles and Their Effects. Parenting For Brain. https://www.parentingforbrain.com/4-baumrind-parenting-styles/

Mandel, L. (2019, June 13). Why We Need Friends, According To A Scientist. The FADER. https://www.thefader.com/2017/03/08/science-of-friendship

Marketing. (2020, November 29). Codependents & Boundaries: Why Do They Struggle? PIVOT. https://www.lovetopivot.com/what-cause-triggers-codependency-boundaries-recovery-coaching/

Morin, A. (2020, October 26). Strategies That Will Help You Become More Authoritative to Your Kids. Verywell Family. https://www.verywellfamily.com/ways-to-become-a-more-authoritative-parent-4136329

Newman, L. (2015, March 6). *When To Say Yes: What To Ask Before You Agree To Something.* HuffPost. https://www.huffpost.com/entry/when-to-say-yes-agree_n_1930507

Patterson, E. (2020, November 6). *Stress Statistics.* The Recovery Village Drug and Alcohol Rehab. https://www.therecoveryvillage.com/mental-health/stress/related/stress-statistics/

Psychologists Explain How to Stay Calm In An Argument. (2020, September 25). Power of Positivity: Positive Thinking & Attitude. https://www.powerofpositivity.com/psychologists-explain-stay-calm-argument/

RAINN. (n.d.). *Victims of Sexual Violence: Statistics | RAINN.* Rainn. Org. https://www.rainn.org/statistics/victims-sexual-violence

Raypole, C. (2019, December 12). *What Makes a Relationship Healthy?* Healthline. https://www.healthline.com/health/healthy-relationship#characteristics

Rees, C. (2020, November 3). *Setting Boundaries in a Codependent Relationship.* THE LOVE BRAIN. https://thelovebrain.com/2020/09/28/setting-boundaries-in-a-codependent-relationship/

ROBBINS RESEARCHINTERNATIONAL, INC. (2020, December 17). *<i>10 steps for how to overcome fear and achieve goals.* Tonyrobbins.Com. https://www.tonyrobbins.com/stories/unleash-the-power/overcoming-fear-in-5-steps/</div>

Saviuc, L. D. (2020, January 7). *On Living Life like a Human Being, Not a Human Doing.* Purpose Fairy. https://www.purposefairy.com/82716/living-life-like-human-being-not-human-doing/

Setting Boundaries. (2019). The Therapist Aid. https://www.therapistaid.com/worksheets/setting-boundaries.pdf

Shebloski, B. (2005, December 1). APA PsycNet. APA PsycNet. https://doi.apa.org/doiLanding?doi=10.1037%2F0893-3200.19.4.633

Siefert, R. (2020, February 10). Relationship Boundaries You Might Not Realize You're Violating. The Active Times. https://www.theactivetimes.com/violating-relationship-boundaries/slide-6

Stines, S. P. (2019, August 18). Setting Boundaries with a Narcissist. Psych Central. https://psychcentral.com/pro/recovery-expert/2019/08/setting-boundaries-with-a-narcissist#4

Tawwab, N. G. (2021). Set Boundaries, Find Peace. TaracherPerigee/Piatus.

Touroni, E. (2020, August 6). How to stand up for yourself (and why you find it so difficult). The Chelsea Psychology Clinic. https://www.thechelseapsychologyclinic.com/uncategorised/how-to-stand-up-for-yourself/

Vision Psychology. (2020, October 22). Setting Boundaries with your Mother-in-Law - Hannah Jensen-Fielding | Vision Psychology Brisbane. https://www.visionpsychology.com/setting-boundaries-with-mother-in-law/

Well, T., Ph. D. (2018, January 29). How to Nonverbally Communicate Openness and Set Boundaries. Psychology Today. https://www.psychologytoday.com/us/blog/the-clarity/201801/how-nonverbally-communicate-openness-and-set-boundaries

Why Setting Boundaries with a Verbally Abusive Partner Is Okay |

HealthyPlace. (2020, June 3). [Video]. YouTube. https://www.
youtube.com/watch?v=TI8d0DE3NzM

wikiHow. (2021, May 6). How to Cope with Mean Parents in the
Long Term. https://www.wikihow.com/Cope-with-Mean-Parents-
in-the-Long-Term

Wikipedia contributors. (2021, May 8). Body language. Wikipedia.
https://en.wikipedia.org/wiki/Body_language